Get Organized

D1591108

Get Organized

How to Clean Up Your Messy Digital Life

Jill Duffy

PC Mag
New York, NY

Contents

Foreword

There's no other way of saying it: I wanted to write this book.

I was going to call it *Power Tools: Save Time, Save Money, and Get More Done*. It was going to be a technologist's guide to productivity. We review thousands of products and services at PC Magazine and I read (almost) every one of those reviews. With this vast knowledge base, getting enough material for a book would be easy. All I needed was an extra hour a day, plus a few weekends without watching football. Piece of cake. There was just one small problem: I'm not very organized.

I fake it pretty well. My office, for example, is clean and remarkably free of clutter. Seriously, people remark on it. Open a desk drawer, however, and you'll find a tangled mess of spare change, business cards, napkins, ink cartridges, a Cholula Hot Sauce packet, seven USB keys, and three keys to locks that are a complete mystery to me. I try to avoid paper files whenever possible, but what I must keep gets stored in the same filing system that I've used for the last 15 years. I call it Alpha 26. Twenty-six file folders labeled A through Z. Invoices? File under I. Taxes? T. It works. Mostly.

My digital life isn't any better, although technology helps me fake it there, too. I can search through my entire digital history, but most of the time I have no idea where the files actually are. Like everyone, I struggle with email. I only check my personal account every few days, but I received 287 emails yesterday on my work account alone. (And this is after SaneLater and my spam filter removed about 200 emails.) There is no way I can read them all and get work done, let alone lead a remotely meaningful life. My email management plan consists of three things:

1. Never miss an email from your boss.
2. Delete what you can.
3. Try to keep up.

This is not a strategy that deserves book-length exploration.

Even worse, my lack of organizational skills is compounded by preternatural inclination toward sloth and indolence. I don't want to spend time getting organized, I want to download an app and simply be organized. I've pursued this techno-utopian goal for years. It's why I bought the Palm Treo 650 as soon as it came out. It's why I keep renewing my Evernote Premium subscription even though I never use it. It's why I pay SaneLater $5.79 to police my inbox even though I already have a corporate spam filter. Surely the next version, with just a few new features, will finally help me get a handle on this mixed-up mess of a digital life.

This will not happen—to me or anyone else. As good as these tools are, they aren't enough to change your life. For that, you need to change yourself. More specifically, you have to change what you do. Jill Duffy taught me that.

When Jill interviewed for a position at *PC Magazine*, she threw in as an aside: "People say I'm the most organized person they know." Organizational skills are a good thing in any profession, but to be honest I was more interested in Jill's writing skills and technical fluency. I knew she was a special talent, but I could not imagine how deeply her organizational prowess would infiltrate her writing and our workplace in general.

Jill's weekly column is one of the most read, and most shared, series on PCMag.com. From naming files on your computer to backing up your digital music library, Jill has collected her best tips and advice in this book. She has also added depth, details, and descriptions that needed to be explored at book length. (Plus, you'll find video tutorials and explanations in several chapters, or links to them if your device does not support video natively.)

With this book, Jill attacks the biggest tech organizational problems we experience at home, at work, and everywhere else. And more important, she delivers concrete solutions that anyone can use. Personally, I think *Get Organized: How to Clean Up Your Messy Digital Life* will prove to be invaluable to anyone who wants to save time, save money, and get more done.

There is just no other way of saying it.

Dan Costa
Editor-in-Chief, *PC Magazine*

Introduction

How do you switch from being a messy person who has piles of papers, an avalanche of reports, and memos overtaking your desk to someone who digitizes files and can find anything with a few quick keyword searches? How do you become someone who always adds meetings and appointments to a calendar and reviews the day's agenda first thing each morning to be prepared when the client wants to see figures, or the doctor asks for the logs you've been keeping of your blood pressure? If you dream of living a life that's better organized, more focused, more in your control, it's probably easier to point out where you're going wrong than figure out what you should be doing that's right. What's harder is answering the questions: How do you get to that more organized place? What steps must you take to change? What do you have to do?

Like so many things in life, the dream of being more organized and resting peacefully each night knowing that everything will now run smoothly is a big fat scam.

Oh, I said it.

Yes, being organized helps tremendously in numerous ways at creating a life that's more likely to go right, and that's better and less stressful than a disorganized one. But don't kid yourself into believing that being organized will solve all your existing problems or prevent new ones in the future. The reason I mention the imperfections of being organized is because this book aims to be one of the most realistic, practical, and levelheaded guidebooks you'll ever read. As such, I want to start out with a crystal-clear discussion of expectations. No gilding the lily. No bullshit. No waxing lyrical about a perfect world.

Being more organized through the methods outlined in this

book will reduce stress, eliminate certain kinds of problems, and make your life easier day in and day out. It will make you feel empowered. It will help you score points at work. It will let you focus on your goals rather than spend all your energy battling daily nonsense. But it won't eliminate every heartache and headache. Life just doesn't work that way.

This ebook is a how-to guide for people looking to increase their organizational habits specifically in and around their technology products. It tackles life both at work and at home, which these days is often the same thing.

If you've ever wished for an empty email inbox or wondered how to best manage hundreds of unlabeled photos on your computer, this book will give you practical guidance, as well as philosophical principles that will steer you toward being in control of your digital life.

The Origins of 'Get Organized'

Get Organized: How to Reclaim Control of Your Messy Digital Life grew out of a weekly column that I write for PCMag.com called simply "Get Organized" (pcmag.com/get-organized). It officially kicked off in January 2012, but the subject matter has been with me much longer than that.

All the concrete tips and logistical advice you'll read in this book come largely from my own personal organizational habits, although many are also influenced by discussions I've had with efficiency experts, software developers of productivity applications, and other organized people. Some of the methods and tricks I use came from colleagues and mentors, some I picked up from other professional sources, such as articles and books, and many others I developed naturally through my own trial and error. Likewise, the founding principles are my own but have been refined through years of practice, thought, and conversations.

Although a lot of what's contained herein is related to white-collar "knowledge work," the foundational points are universally applicable both at home and in an office setting. At times, you might even realize that the guiding advice fits other areas of your life, too, from parenting to managing your own health and fitness.

How we use our computers, smartphones, tablets, software, and so on, isn't just about data. It's about you and your relationship to that data: how and when you use it, how you think about it, and how you prepare yourself for success or failure depending on whether you can align your actions to your thought processes.

A Philosophy of Being Organized

Think for a moment about the most organized person you know. Imagine this person waking up in the morning and going about her day. She makes her bed, brews coffee, eats breakfast, puts on an ironed shirt and slacks, and grabs her car keys from the same spot where she always leaves them every evening. She arrives to work on time, reviews her calendar, looks over her to-do list, and starts knocking off those tasks early. By midday, her desk is still tidy. She's punctual and prepared for meetings. After work she makes time to exercise or go to her kids' after-school activities, and always eats dinner at the table—never standing over the sink. By 11:00, she's in bed, perhaps reading for a few minutes, before getting her seven hours of sleep.

How would you describe this person? Neat and orderly, sure, but what else? Is she trustworthy? Hardworking? Detail-oriented? Efficient? Self-disciplined?

We tend to associate positive and sometimes even moral characteristics to organized people. We believe, whether implicitly or explicitly, that they are committed, honest, reliable, and sometimes just plain good. Organized people make good decisions or "do the right thing." Often we trust them more than disorganized people.

But in reality, being "organized" isn't a character trait at all. It's a state of being that results from actions—what we do, rather than who we are. Someone who is organized might be "calculating" more than efficient and focused, or "ruthless" rather than disciplined.

When we see work getting done on time and on budget, we give the benefit of the doubt to the person who has done it, especially if that person is consistent in his or her behavior. I believe that culturally we've adopted a stereotype of organized people—an overwhelmingly positive one. Often we believe that organized people are just born that way, that they're good people, and that their organizational habits come from a strong sense of responsibility and moral goodness. Again, I don't think it's explicit at all, and in fact if you question someone about these beliefs, the sheer act of verbalizing it unravels the assumptions pretty quickly. But by and large, we don't really question it.

I for one have benefited tremendously from this assumption and stereotype. My own journey to becoming an organized person didn't originate from a moral high ground in the slightest. In fact, it started as a coping mechanism that I developed after growing up in a highly dysfunctional household. My family was poor and faced a lot of problems related to being poor that compounded one another. I could see that there wasn't one big problem but rather a hundred little ones that were difficult to fix because they all interlaced.

The moment I left the house and went out into the world on my own, I became not only highly organized for the first time in my life, but also somewhat obsessed with having self-control—a negative quality, definitely, but one that was easily masked by those positive stereotypes related to being organized.

And yet, I benefited hugely. My professors, bosses, and peers saw an organized, efficient, detail-oriented student, employee, and housemate. I wrote for the university newspaper and was promoted quickly. I was elected president of a student club. I mostly got A grades. Inside, though, I was coping with the stresses of a supremely dysfunctional childhood.

I've since found more balance in life, and a lot of that balance I now attribute to understanding the difference between being organized and being productive.

Organization vs. Productivity

A perennial problem of highly organized people, which can go unnoticed to others, is that we can and sometimes do get distracted by our own need to be organized. If you've ever wasted five minutes rearranging the dishwasher to fit two more cups into the top rack, you know what I mean.

A personal example I like to share happens whenever I have to buy a lot of groceries, such as for a party. As I make my way from the produce to the meats to the canned goods, I pull over in the aisles practically every 30 feet to rearrange my shopping cart. The cans must be stacked neatly on the bottom. Cold items should be clustered together. I like the boxes all standing straight upward and facing the same direction.

But organizing a shopping cart is completely pointless and a waste of time. The moment I reach the checkout counter (which would have been 50 minutes sooner had I not been rearranging my cart every other minute), I have to stack everything onto the conveyor belt and watch helplessly as the cashier sweeps my groceries into a new messy pile on the other end. Then I once again step in and say, "No, no. I'll bag my own stuff!" so that I can once again rearrange everything... even though within ten minutes I'll be home and unpacking, which is to say undoing all the work I just did. It's a rabbit hole. There's no return on investment (ROI), as it were. It's organizing for organization's sake without any benefit or payout.

What I'm hinting at here is the difference between being "organized" and being "productive." It's very possible to be organized without being productive, as in the case of rearranging the items in a shopping cart. But it's difficult to be productive without being at least a little bit organized.

Productive moments happen when we focus on the right things—that is, the things that benefit our work or personal lives, the things that have high ROI. In the digital world, one area where people often focus on the wrong things is in email, particularly in spending a lot of time trying to craft language just so and write perhaps several paragraphs' worth of material when three or four sentences would have done just fine, and probably with greater clarity. I see the same wasted effort in college students who spend 30 or 40 minutes adjusting the format and font on their papers. If only they had spent that time instead hammering out their ideas.

Throughout this book, I'll try to explicitly name the topics on which we should be focusing for the maximum benefit and where we should not be wasting our time and effort. The awareness alone can cause dramatic improvements in one's habits.

Organization as a Lifestyle

Speaking of habits, it's important to consider how being organized is part of a lifestyle, rather than an action you perform once to correct a mess. I like to think of being organized as similar to being fit and healthy. The word "diet," in its truest sense, refers to what we eat day in and day out over a long period of time, not what we ate today or even just this week. Our health is also shaped by how much activity we get over our lifetime, not a few weeks' worth of jogging or hitting the gym. Diet and fitness are defined by years upon years of actions, not what we do for a limited time only. Being organized is the same.

With digital organization, we might take the example of cleaning out our email inbox. I routinely keep only about a single screen's worth of emails, but sometimes that slips and I get behind so that there may be a scrolling list of stuff in my inbox that I haven't conquered yet. The next day, it's a little bit harder to process emails, but the day after that it gets better, and within three days, everything's back to normal.

In some sense, you might think of "being organized" as a series of habits and routines, rather than a finished outcome. Being organized is "filing away each scrap of paper as it accumulates" rather than "having a clean desk." Being organized is "naming and tagging photo files when they're uploaded" rather than "having rearranged hundreds of wedding photos." The first is a set of consistent behaviors while the second is a one-off project.

Occasionally we have to take on one-off projects in order to process a backlog of work or overhaul some problem, but in the long run the only true way to stay organized is to make it part of your lifestyle. There's greater payoff in having rules that you follow consistently and regularly rather than massive projects or piles of work that you try to conquer twice a year.

Realistic Expectations

I worry sometimes that people believe that being organized will solve their problems at work or in their home lives. I worry that people imagine that scheduling every soccer game and school activity on a family calendar will make them a better parent. I worry that someone who rearranges a spice cupboard will believe she'll thereafter be a better and more frequent home cook. That's not what organization does, and it's important to think through, realistically, what you can expect from being more organized.

Will it help you be on time for appointments and meetings more often? Yes. Will it help you find the things you need quickly and efficiently? Yes. Will it change the quality of your work or personal life or parenting? Probably not. What it will do is make it easier for you to improve your work. It will create an environment that's supportive of your doing well. It paves the way for possibilities and often reduces the amount of effort needed to achieve whatever it is you want.

Those benefits are by no means trivial. In fact, they are crucial. As I said earlier, to be productive, you must be at least a little bit organized. One supports the other. Organization enables productivity, but it doesn't make it happen. You make it happen. But being organized is the health and fitness lifestyle that creates possibilities. And as you develop organized habits and they turn into an organized lifestyle, you may find you don't even have to think about what steps you need to take or what rules you need to follow to achieve your goals. That kind of stuff falls into place easily when you're organized.

A Bit About This Book

Although the chapters of this book are structured such that you can skip around and read the relevant sections, you'll likely get more value out of it if you read through the whole thing once in order first.

Part I, "Getting Started," covers many of the grounding philosophies behind why being organized is important—and not just for the outcomes, but also because of the way in which other people perceive you when you show traits of an organized person. It's also about a few basic pieces of technology: your computer and its desktop, as well as the folders and files that reside on it.

Part II focuses on online computing, which includes Web-based services such as online email. It contains an in-depth chapter on email management, a tortuous topic for many people. Part II also has chapters on passwords for your online accounts and how to manage them in a way that's both secure and sane, storage and back-up, and what you need to know about "the cloud."

Part III embraces smartphones, exploring all the functions and apps you can use to better organize your life with these handy and ever-present devices. It also contains detailed tips on how to maintain a smartphone so that it stays free of junk but always has what you need.

Lastly, Part IV more generally touches on a few other personal topics related to our digital lives, such as social media, personal finance, music, and preparing your accounts and passwords to be passed on when you die. That last one is not a happy subject, I know, but it is important for those people in charge to taking over your affairs after your death.

A few other notes: The "work" mentioned throughout in this book encompasses not just on-the-job work, but also tasks related to your digital life at home (such as managing your digital music collection). When a topic or piece of advice specifically relates to the office environment, though, you'll see a callout for **BUSI-NESS.**

At the end of some chapters, you'll see Additional Content, sections containing more detailed information about a particular topic.

And along the way, look for prompts that will lead you to companion videos, too.

No matter how little or how much you hope to reorganize your life, I sincerely hope that this book gives you straightforward advice and clearly explained steps for implementation. And sure, not everyone will follow my exact guidelines at every turn, but if you understand the foundation and purpose behind the methods, you can easily tweak the implementation to better suit you.

Jill Duffy

I

Part I: Getting Started

1

Where to Start

The crux of your digital life is likely your computer, whether it's a laptop at home or a desktop computer at the office. It doesn't matter if it's a Mac or a Windows PC, or if you have multiple machines. The computer itself is where we'll start.

In this chapter, I'll first give you a quick and dirty solution for cleaning up any computer that's "messy" in the most general sense. It only takes a few minutes, and I'll explain the theory behind why you would want to do it.

From there, I'll explain a few other basic safeguards and "cleaning" tools that will help you keep your computer in good working order. This chapter isn't an in-depth explanation of machine maintenance. Rather, it's a high-level overview for keeping your computer more organized.

I. HOW TO CLEAN UP A DESKTOP

When you open or boot up your computer, what's the first thing you see? The desktop.

The computer desktop is a focal point. Think of it as the mother of all home screens, the place where you return when you need to reorient yourself or pause between tasks. It's where you take a breath to recuperate, if only for a moment, and think about your next step. (Some people feel the same way about the My Documents area or "Name" area in Mac OS, and that's fine. This clean-up job works in those locations, too.)

Because the desktop is so important, I highly recommend minimalism. I like my desktop to be very clean and clear of clutter. I only want to see files, folders, and program icons that are relevant to what I need to get done. I don't want to see any surprises or messes when I visit my desktop in between tasks, during those crucial moments when I'm refocusing my mind before going onto the next thing.

If your desktop is a disaster—a smattering of files and shortcuts and folders and icons—you probably don't see it as a rejuvenating place. That's a major hindrance to your productivity, but it's not irreversible. Let's fix it right now in approximately two to five minutes by "sweeping" it.

Step 1: Create Year Folders

First create a few folders on the desktop (or the My Documents area, or wherever your central place of focus may be), and name them by year. Start with the current year, and create five folders total, working backward. For example, you should have folders called 2013, 2012, 2011, 2010, and 2009. If the year system doesn't make sense based on the files you have at hand, you could also create month folders, which I would recommend naming with a four-digit number at the start, followed by the month name, such that August 2013 would be "1308_August." (Chapters 2 and 3 go into a lot more detail about this numerical convention.)

If the messy files on your desktop go back further in time than that, just call the earliest folder "2008 and older" (or whatever is the applicable year). Windows 8 users may want to see the Additional Content at the end of this chapter that dives into organizing the app icons on the Windows Home Screen.

Step 2: Sort Files by Date

Next, sort all your desktop files by year.

For beginners: In Mac OS X use the Finder, or in Windows a new window with desktop as the selected location, and then click to sort by date.

Watch:

"How to Sweep a Desktop,"
part of the Get Organized Video Series
at bit.ly/DesktopSweep

Step 3: Sweep

Finally, move all the files that were created or last edited (whichever you prefer) into the year specified to the appropriate folder.

For beginners: Select the first file, hold the Shift key, and then click the last file in question; this automatically selects everything in between. See the video.

Do the same thing with any stray folders on your desktop. Shuffle them into the applicable year folder.

Tip:

When I'm working on a lot of different files at once,
I sometimes create a folder called INBOX that I only
intend to keep temporarily. It's where I put files that
are immediate and important right now, but that I will
file away later. Just be sure you make it a habit to move
those files to a more appropriate location later.

Purpose of a Sweep

The purpose of this exercise is to simply reclaim your desktop. As you may have just experienced, it takes no time at all, even for novices. Your files are still there, completely available to you, but your desktop is now much less cluttered.

As mentioned, Windows users might find all these same ideas apply inside the My Documents folder. Mac users can apply these concepts to their Documents or user folder. You can even "sweep" your email inbox. That's all well and good, but I really do think that cleaning up the desktop environment is extremely important.

You can keep all your year folders right on your desktop, or further nest them by dragging them another area, such as My Documents. It's entirely up to you. Some technical people might argue that the latter option is more in line with how the operating system itself is meant to be used, although I think it's perfectly fine to keep things on the desktop if that's where you like them and it helps you stay organized and focused.

How Does a Clean Desktop Look?

A clean desktop should have maybe a dozen or so items on it, including a few local folders or shortcuts to them. Your desktop might also have a handful of "working files," meaning files that are actively in progress and that you haven't yet filed to an appropriate folder. The desktop might also contain a few shortcuts to network locations (e.g., shared folders on a server) and, in Windows XP, frequently used programs. On a Mac, frequently used programs will appear in the applications bar. Windows 7 and 8 users can pin their favorite programs to the taskbar and Start screen, respectively.

Figure 1-1: A clean desktop should have a minimal number of files, folders and shortcuts on it to help you stay focused between tasks. Keeping a few works in progress on the desktop is a fine idea; they will be highly visible and grab your attention, encouraging you to focus on the right things.

You might have a widget or two as well, but they shouldn't be distracting. The desktop serves its purpose best when you keep it minimal so that it can act as a place to focus and reorient yourself throughout the day while you're working.

With a clean and tidy desktop, you're able to set forth with a new system for how you will work from here on out. As I mentioned in the Introduction to this book, the system you design must be built on solid habits you will practice day in and day out.

The next few chapters in Part I outline in great detail a system for computer organization that works for many people. Feel free to adapt it based on your specific needs, including the kind of work you do, the people with whom you collaborate, and most important, the way you personally think about your data. If you develop habits and a system that meet your personality and preferences, you're more likely to stick to them, which is crucial to success.

II. ADD PROTECTION THROUGH UNIQUE USER ACCOUNTS

If you share a computer with other people, as is the case with many family computers, you'll need to create different user accounts. Each person will be able to log in to his or her own account so that they don't mess up your files as you begin to organize them. Of course, having separate user accounts also gives you and your family members more privacy, and lets you put in place parental controls or other user limitations should you need them.

Security and Antivirus

Before you set up any user accounts, though, be sure your Windows PC or Mac has basic security software installed. If it already does, skip ahead to the next section.

A lot of very good antivirus software is free, and sometimes it even comes preinstalled. But you might want something more than this basic protection, especially if children will be using your computer.

AVG Family Safety is a really good choice; though it's not free, it does give parents the ability to check in on their kids' computer use from any Web-enabled device. It lets you set time limits for computer use, too. And it has some good features for blocking access to potentially harmful websites via your wireless router rather than the computer itself so kids can't get around these restrictions by using other Internet-enabled devices, such as smartphones and video game consoles.

Setting Up Accounts and Logins

With a shared computer, every user should have his or her own login. Additionally, I recommend setting up a "Guest" account that visitors can use, but that also lets family members get onto the machine in a pinch if they forget their passwords.

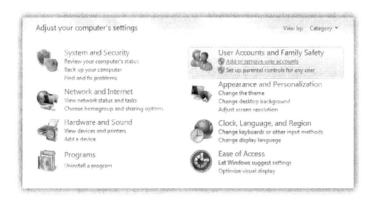

Figure 1-2: You can set up new user accounts in Windows from the User ACcounts and Family Safety section of the Control Panel.

Here's how to create new user accounts:

Windows: In the User Accounts and Family Safety section of the control panel, click on User Accounts, then Manage another account, then Create a new account. From there, it's just a matter of following the prompts. Windows 7 will ask if you want to use Windows Live Family Safety to set up the controls, in which case you'll have to connect to the Internet and login with a Windows Live ID (which could take more time if you need to set one up), but you can still manage a lot of basic features right in the system, if you prefer.

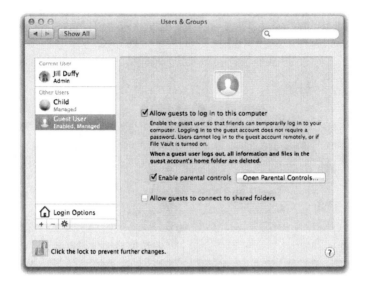

Figure 1-3: In Mac OS X, you can create new user accounts, including a guest user account, which is useful for visitors or when a family member forgets his or her password.

<u>Mac OS X:</u> Go to System Preferences and look for Users & Groups. Click the plus sign to add a new account, then just follow the prompts. To enable restrictions on the different accounts, go back to the System Preferences and jump into Parental Controls. There you'll find tools for setting time limits, blocking websites, and enabling other restrictions.

Remote Access

Another consideration: If you want to be able to help family members with their computer skills or troubleshoot problems (either theirs or yours) without any awkward phone calls, you need to set up remote access. Remote access lets a person drive one computer from a different computer, even one that's thousands of miles away. In other words, if you hit a problem with your computer that you just can't fix, you could call up your sister and ask her to log in to the remote access program to literally take over your computer from her house, even if she lives across the country. Conversely, if your uncle routinely calls you up for tech advice, you could fix his problems for him rather than talk him through it.

Remote access tools are a dime a dozen. The one you choose will depend on the operating systems of the machines you need to connect, and whether an experienced person will be setting up the controls on both machines (some remote access tools are kinder on the less technical among us than others).

You can connect two Windows PC fairly easily using Microsoft's Remote Desktop, which generally comes included on Windows computers. This option will probably work best when a more experienced user is setting up remote access on both machines. VNC is a good free option for connecting two computers running different operating systems, such as OS X and Windows. Again, this method works best if the more experienced person can install the necessary components first.

Two other options that are easier for less-experienced people to set up are LogMeIn (free and paid Pro versions available) and TeamViewer (free). Both programs work across multiple operating systems, and they have mobile apps for iOS and Android, too.

III. INSTALL A TUNE-UP UTILITY

There are other ways to keep a computer "clean" other than simply sweeping your desktop, and generally speaking, it's more efficient to let a program do this work for you than try to do it yourself by hand.

If your computer has ever acted sluggish, the root problem may have been that a lot of little problems built up, such as having duplicate files, unneeded downloads, and the remnants of programs that never uninstalled properly. A tune-up utility cleans out all this garbage and tidies up a few other areas that help the machine run smoother and more reliably.

In many ways, tuning up a PC keeps it internally "organized." Essential data is filed away appropriately. Junk gets tossed. And parts of the system that were starting to get messy or torn apart (fragmented) are patched back together again.

Most tune-ups do the following (don't sweat it if you don't know what all these things mean):

- defragment the driverepair in the system Registry
- delete unnecessary and duplicate files
- uninstall and remove programs that did not properly uninstall previously
- check for driver updates
- remove data that you don't need related to your Internet browsers

Two good tune-up utilities are Iolo System Mechanic and SlimWare Utilities SlimCleaner. I use a free tune-up utility on my Mac called CCleaner. With most tune-up utilities, you can set them to run automatically every day or once a month—however often you want—or you can just press a button to make them run when you think it's time for a little automatic cleanup.

Monthly checklist: Run your tune-up utility at least once a month. You can open the utility to initiate the process yourself, or schedule tune-ups to occur once a month automatically in the software of your choice.

There are a lot of other essential programs and services that you can and should install on your computer, such as backup services, file-syncing programs, and a password manager; I'll explore these in later chapters. For now, your computer should be in much better shape both on the technical side and for you on the psychological side. With a clean and clutter-free desktop, you'll be able to focus on other tasks that you want to complete, whether it's organizing your folders and files (the topic of the next two chapters), or just getting general work done.

IV. TAKE-AWAYS

- Your computer desktop should be an uncluttered area of focus.
- Create folders named by year, such as 2010, 2011, and 2012, and sweep any messy desktop files into those folders based on when they were created or last edited.
- A clean desktop should contain essential shortcuts for programs, network locations, and no more than a handful of "working files," or work that is current and in progress.
- On any shared computer, setting up different user accounts will help keep your files organized by preventing other people from getting at them; they are also helpful for parental controls.
- Remote desktop software helps less technical people get computer help from their more experienced friends and family from afar.
- Install a tune-up utility to keep your computer clean in ways that are difficult to do by hand.

V. Recommended Tools and Services

- AVG Family Safety
- CCleaner
- Iolo System Mechanic

- LogMeIn
- Microsoft's Remote Desktop
- SlimWare Utilities SlimCleaner
- TeamViewer
- VNC

- Additional Content -

Organizing Tiles in Windows 8

Windows 8's user interface looks remarkably different from those in prior versions of Windows. Instead of clicking on desktop icons to get to your favorite programs, you'll find "tiles" on a new Start screen. You can rearrange these tiles just as you can organize app icons on most smartphones. Here are some tips and ideas for how to do it.

Be sure to download and install apps before organizing existing ones. The reason? Apps can be different sizes: Some may be one-by-one squares, others rectangular and twice as wide as they are tall. You can shrink a rectangular tile to the square dimensions to make it fit more neatly if you like, but you can't always expand a square to the rectangular shape. Plopping a double-wide tile into an organized set can throw the whole thing off. So try to get a bunch of tiles on your plate before you start moving them around.

When you're ready to start rearranging the placement of your tiles, use one of these three methods:

- **Hotspots:** Put high-use apps onto "hotspots" of the screen, or areas where you're likely to put your fingers or reach with your mouse first. For many touch screen users, the hotspots are the vertical areas along the left and right sides, near your thumbs when you're holding the device.

- **Grid:** Put apps in a grid formation, left to right and top to bottom.
- **Cluster by workflow:** Group apps into sets based on your own common workflows. For example, set together Word, Excel, PowerPoint, and a "print management" tile, or leisure apps like games and Web discovery tools. You can name sets to help you remember the idea behind your groups.Organizing Tiles in Windows 8_

2

How to Find Everything

Now that you have a tidy desktop, containing nothing more than a few folders named by years and perhaps a couple of shortcuts to programs or shared locations, we can really get down to business. Before you can make much headway in terms of reorganizing all your files, you need to figure out just how you think about information.

I. HOW DO YOU THINK ABOUT YOUR DATA?

The way you think about "information," from text files to family photos to spreadsheets of quarterly earnings, will largely determine how you organize your computer. After all, the whole reason you're organizing your computer is so you can find files faster. You want to be able to pull up presentations and look up facts and figures quickly without having to think about where they are.

When you cultivate a lifestyle of digital organization the locations of files and other information becomes intuitive. You always know exactly where information lives. But the framework is not the same for everyone.

Context Matters

The way you personally think about information is contextual. Is your work divided into projects or by client? Is it thematically arranged?

For me as a writer, everything I work on is tied to a date. I typically remember when something published above all else. Whenever I look up an article, I always see a publish date at the top of it. So I organize all my files by date. That's how I think about my information.

How *you* think about your information will depend on your job, your personal preferences, and possibly other factors that I cannot predict. It's entirely dependent on your personal context. For example, some writers remember articles they write based on the topic rather than the publishing date, particularly long-form writers whose articles or books might span months or years from development to publication. Other businesspeople tell me that the client name or project name is what becomes important. Some people, especially in the financial sector, work on a quarterly system, so the quarter is how they remember things.

The Year-Month System

My work folders are structured into a year-month system, which uses a two-digit year and two-digit month, so that April 2013 becomes 1304. On my computer I have a series of nested folders—for example, a 2013 folder with subfolders whose names begin with 1301 (for January), 1302 (February), 1303, and so on. In this chapter, I'll explain in depth how I set up these folders and what value I get from the method I use.

One huge reason I like and trust in the four-digit year-month system (sometimes it's even a six-digit year-month-date system; see Chapter 3) is it keeps folder names unique. If you have two folders called "June," it's entirely possible to make a mistake and overwrite files, especially in a business environment with a shared server! On the other hand, if you have one folder called "1306_JUN" and another called "1206_JUN," it's impossible to accidentally overwrite any of the information contained therein.

Just because I use a year-month system doesn't mean you

should, however. Many of the reasons it works so well for me have to do with the fact that I remember chronology, and that every single one of my articles ever published has a publish date attached to it. Your context is likely different. I will explain the "why" behind the system, though, so that you can adapt it to better suit your own needs.

II. THE BUSINESS CASE

Before you read on, remember that being organized has to be a lifestyle commitment. That's a simple analogy to make for individuals, but it becomes much trickier when we're talking about an entire business and staff. I imagine a lot of people reading this book are interested in organizing not just their own personal computer and smartphone, but also their office computer and work-related gadgets, too. And indeed, there's a lot of good content in here that's specific to small business owners and even team leaders of larger organization.

The biggest difference between your own personal devices and those you use for business is collaboration. At home, you might be the only person who ever looks at your files. You're the only one digging through that photo collection trying to find the picture of Grandpa Jones eating ice cream cake on his 90th birthday. But in an office setting, many people often need access to the same files. Even if your work is fairly autonomous, you probably have some IT professional overseeing your machine, or an accountant who will at some point need to sort through some spreadsheets and invoices. And when you eventually leave the company, someone else may have to inherit your files.

In a business or professional organization, every employee and stakeholder in the day-to-day operations has to be able to stick to the program of keeping files and folders neat. The organizational system has to consist of practices that fit into everyone's routines, whether it means taking small steps consistently, such as deleting unnecessary files as you go, or taking larger steps on a regimented schedule, such as reserving every Friday afternoon for cleaning out inboxes.

So before you put yourself and your coworkers on a new diet for being organized, take a moment to think about how your business views its information.

Matching Practices to Reality

In a business, it's extremely important to not force some organizational system onto all the employees if it doesn't reflect how the team actually operates. Ask your employees or colleagues, "If you needed to find a particular document, maybe an invoice or a contract, where would you look first?" And, more importantly, "How would you look?"

Do people search their computers or the company's network by vendor name, date, or product description? Do they open a folder and skim filenames, or sort by date, or sort by file type? How long does it take them to find the information? Are they wasting time because they're searching in a way that doesn't help them narrow down their results quickly?

You don't need a formal meeting to find out answers to these questions. Just drop by and ask the people who do the hands-on work. It will take a few minutes at most. (As an aside, I believe business managers should do this kind of exercise—asking their employees how they work and how they think—once or twice a year. If you're out of touch with how the people on the ground think and work from a process point of view, you will be totally lost in terms of appropriately giving them the tools they need to effectively grow the business.)

Regarding the question about how you or your employees think about data, there may be more than one answer. At times, you might remember the month and year in which a project launched, while your colleague remembers instead the name of the project. And in both cases, the information isn't necessarily static. What if the project had a code name during development and a different name at launch? How do you implement a system that can handle these kinds of incongruities?

Thinking about how you and your colleagues look for information should help shape your understanding of how you or your business should structure its information—but sleep on it for a day or two. Sometimes we forget why certain practices are in place, and changing them abruptly could inadvertently destroy some other logic or business rationale.

III. HOW TO SET UP A FOLDER STRUCTURE

Folders form the skeleton of your data and files, whether they're for personal use or business. Like a building's structure, folders support everything else that goes up around them, from creative design to straightforward functionality. To be effective, they should represent your workflow. In other words, they should logically mirror whatever it is you do with the work you create.

Watch:

"Why Folder Structure Matters,"
part of the Get Organized Video Series
at bit.ly/FolderStructureMatters

The system you design for your folder structure might also be the exact same one you end up using to manage email (see Chapter 4) or on a shared server in an office, although it doesn't have to be. It all depends on what you do with those kinds of files and pieces of communication.

BUSINESS: I've worked in several different office environments over the course of my career. The teams that had clean folder structures built on commonsense ideas were always the ones best positioned for continued success and growth. Small business owners should note that fact: An organized company is one that's positioned for growth. You may think that because there are only two people in the company now, you can keep a lot of information in your head and not map it to a folder structure. Unfortunately, when it's time to hire new employees and grow your business, you'll waste a lot of time teaching them your convoluted system. You'll waste even more time and money correcting mistakes.

What Are Folders, Really?

Your folder structure is a reflection of your working structure or your business. Folders are nested within other folders in a hierarchical system that needs to match the hierarchical order of your processes.

In the previous section, I asked you to think about your data, or in the case of a business, talk about how you and others in your business think about information. You probably started to see a hierarchy of some kind unfold, one idea nested within another.

I recommend sketching out that structure. It doesn't matter if you sketch it on paper, in bullet points, in a note-taking application, or using mind-mapping software. Just get it down where you can literally see it differently. Putting it in writing will help you spot inconsistencies and overlaps.

Example Folder Structure

The structure of your design will be unique, but because it helps tremendously to see an example, I'll show you the basic one that I use on my desktop.

In my work with PCMag.com, I primarily write product

reviews. I test products, rate them against others, and write up my findings. When I think about reviews, I see three categories in my mind's eye:

- ideas for products to review
- articles that are in progress (products that I'm currently testing or have already tested, and that now have an article in draft or the editing stage)
- completed reviews (meaning work that's already published)

Within the "completed" category, I tend to remember reviews by their publication dates, which I simplify to month and year because there are never too many within a single month that I would lose sight of them.

For articles in progress, I typically remember the name of the product first—that's the first thing that comes to mind if someone asks me about products I am in the process of reviewing. The second thing that comes to mind is their proposed date of publication, and you'll see how those two things play out in a moment. But notice how dates are already very important to me and how I think about my information.

Within the "ideas" category, things are much more fluid. Some ideas encompass a category of products, such as "fitness gadgets," while others relate to a single product. But just because they're fluid doesn't mean I can't have a system for keeping them organized.

So, how does this translate to folders?

On my desktop, I have two primary folders for working files:

- Reviews
- Features, Columns, News

You'll remember from Chapter 1 that the desktop should be an area of focus, which is why I keep a highly simplified folder structure here.

Within the Reviews folder, I have a number of folders labeled as past years:

- Reviews
    - 2011
    - 2012

Then I have a number of folders for the current year, drilled down by month. The setup looks something like this:

- Reviews
    - 1301_JAN
    - 1302_FEB
    - 1303_MAR
    - 1304_APR
    - 1305_MAY
    - 2011_Reviews
    - 2012_Reviews

If you were to look inside the folders for 2011 and 2012, you'd see similar year-month subfolders, but I've swept them into a year folder to get them out of sight. (Eventually, I'll archive the files in those past years and move them off my local drive.)

Figure 2-1: In this example folder structure, work is divided by date, or more specifically, by month

Day in and day out, I work in the current year-month folder. In fact, opening that folder is one of the first things I do in the morning when I sit down in front of my machine.

For example, in May 2013, the folder I open first when I get to work is 1305_MAY. It's my go-to location. I never have to even think about where to go. I know all my current projects are there.

Within each year-month folder, I have a final set of folders named after products that I am in the process of reviewing:

- Reviews
  - 1305_MAY
    - Cloze (iPhone app)
    - Duolingo (Android app)
    - EasilyDo (Android app)
    - Fitbit Flex
    - Focus@Will
    - Mailbox (iPad app)

This system works because I see a snapshot of ideas and things in progress every time I open my go-to folder. A complete overview of my work for the month is right there in the name of the folders. My eyes can scan the list of work in progress, and I know immediately what's happening in the current month. I even use custom icons on Windows and color-coding on Mac to get even more information at a glance when I open my go-to folder—see the Additional Content at the end of the chapter.

Another reason my system is efficient for me is because making changes is quick and simple. Let's say the end of May rolls around and I haven't finished two or three reviews. I can simply drag the folders for those reviews into the next month. My basic work outline is then already in place for June.

Folder Tips and Tricks

Here are a few other tips and tricks I use to keep my folders organized.

Numbers. Notice how in my system the year-month folders start with four digits (two digits for the year, two digits for the month), but then I also use an underscore to write the abbreviation for the month name as well. I do that because I like to see names of the months. For me and the way I think about information, the letters deliver meaning to my brain faster than the digits. But the digits serve a purpose, too: They ensure my folders flow chronologically when I sort alphabetically by name (the default).

"Tags." You can think of the month name that I use as a sort of tag, and depending on how you think about information, tags could be extremely important and useful in your system. Here's an example: Let's say in my line of work I typically wrote 40 product reviews in a month. That would mean I had no fewer than 40 subfolders within each month folder. Forty folders is too many to glance at and gather usable information. So I could adapt my system with tags, such that my subfolders had two designations: one called "IN_" meaning "in progress" and one that used an "X_" meaning "completed."

- Reviews
    - 1305_MAY
        - IN_Cloze (iPhone app)
        - IN_Mailbox (iPad app)
        - X_Duolingo (Android app)
        - X_EasilyDo (Android app)
        - X_Fitbit Flex
        - X_Focus@Will

This method is similar to using color-coding (explained in the Additional Content) except that it also still taps into alphabetical sorting. Notice, for example, that I would choose "X_" instead of "DONE_" for my tag because files that start with "X_" will sort down to the bottom of my window. All the "IN_" files will float to the top where I will see them first.

Special characters. Underscores are my best friends in folder naming conventions. They're clean and keep the text easy to read. Some people use spaces and hyphens in their folder names—it's up to you. Whatever you choose, always stay conscious of how the characters affect alphabetical name sorting. Sometimes I use an underscore at the beginning of a folder name when I always want that folder to appear at the top, like "_NEXT." Then I can easily drag and drop anything that's completed to the top folder. Alternatively, if I wanted it at the bottom, I could name it "z_NEXT."

Consistency is Key

Whatever system you implement, stick to it! Consistency is a key to staying organized.

No one expects you to be perfect. The guidelines here and in future chapters focus on finding solutions that you will actually be able to implement and adhere to in the long term. They allow for mistakes, days when you're too lazy to stay on track, and a lot of flexibility. One day doesn't make or break you. The whole concept is to build habits that have long-term payoff, not short-term disaster scenarios if you slip up a couple of times.

What matters are the small actions that you perform day in and day out, over and over and over again. Your system should take all those "lifestyle" issues into consideration. You're only human. Work comes with mistakes, and that's okay. When you create a system that accounts for imperfection in the short term but still manages to get right what's important for the long term, that's a winning formula.

IV. TAKE-AWAYS

- Sketch out your folder structure before implementing it.
- Organize information hierarchically, thinking about what you will need to see and know in a snapshot view when you look in a folder.
- Use letters, numerals, and special characters in your folder names to get them to appear in an intelligent order.

- Be consistent with naming conventions and processes for using folders.

-

———————

- Additional Content -

What Color Can Do for Your Data

Adding a little color to your computer files and folders does more than just appeal to the eye. It's a terrific way to deliver information extremely efficiently for yourself or your team.

When I first became truly computer literate, I spent a lot of time learning the benefits of a well-organized folder structure, as well as clear and meaningful filenames. And then I added color. When used properly, color-coding your folders helps carry more information by indicating the status of what's inside. We already do something similar in email: Unread messages have bold text, whereas read mail is roman (not bold) or perhaps has a gray background, or both. Visual cues are extremely powerful in helping us absorb information.

The concept couldn't be simpler: Define for yourself meanings for different colors or custom icons. Yellow may mean upcoming work. Green could be work in progress. Red may indicate a project that's important or overdue. Gray could be for folders holding finished work. And color-coding is supremely helpful for collaborative projects, too.

Here's how to do it:

Mac. On a Mac, right-click or hold Ctrl while clicking and simply navigate down to the area for labels.

Windows XP. In Windows XP, right-click on a folder in Windows, select Properties, then the Customize tab, and select Change Icon. You'll see a long list of possible icons. I recommend picking icons you can find and access quickly, as well as images that evoke their intended meanings.

Windows 7. In Windows 7, you'll need a small program to help you add some pizzazz to your folders. Plenty of free downloads exist, including Folder Colorizer and Rainbow Folders.

3

Staying Focused

Once you have a neat desktop and a folder structure in place, you can more easily get down to work, right?

Well, almost. The next logical step in making your computer a more organized place is to come up with a good file-naming convention. Sure, it doesn't sound all that sexy, but having clear, consistent, and meaningful filenames lets you see your files in a new way, interact with them more efficiently, and get to your real tasks faster, instead of procrastinating or getting distracted by files that aren't meaningful at the moment.

Filenames help to keep your work organized in a similar way to folders, only at a slightly different level. As with folder names and structures, filenames should reflect the way you think about your work.

Any time you need to find a file you should be able to do so within seconds. That efficiency alone is a huge reason to have an organized computer with clear folder structures and consistent and logical filenames in the first place.

Folders help to segment and organize your workload into groups, whether those groups relate to the months of the year, client names, or projects. A filename just drills down one more level, but should also express additional information about the file, giving you an intuitive sense of what's inside before you even open it.

Try to guess what these files contain:

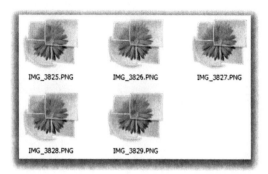

Figure 3-1: Without clear file names, sometimes it's impossible to tell what might be contained inside a file.

You can tell they are image files, but you don't know anything more about them, except maybe to guess the order in which the images were shot. You'd have to open them or inspect their meta-data to find out more.

Now, let me give you a sneak peek at some of my files and their names so you can see what I mean about what clear filenames do:

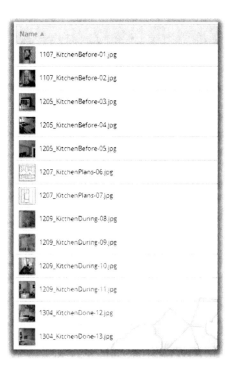

Figure 3-2: Clear and consistently labeled files can tell you a lot about what's in them, which makes finding information you want or need much more efficient.

Look at how much information you can probably figure out just by the names and icons, without ever opening them. You can tell they're images by the JPG extension and by the thumbnail icon. You might have also guessed that these are photos of a kitchen remodeling project "before," "during," and after, or when it was all "done."

Really good filenames simply add more information to the file extension and icon, and thus more value.

When you can see the files and understand what they contain without even opening them, it's much easier to maintain focus on whatever it is you set out to do. The moment you have to open files—or even start reading the files' names—you're ripe for being distracted. If you can scan or skim filenames, you can more quickly target the ones you actually want. These tiny efficiencies add up to leading a more organized life overall. Sometimes it's hard to recognize that fact unless you're in it, though. But trust me: You can get there.

So what do you have to do to get great filenames that in effect make your time in front of a computer more efficient?

I. REQUIREMENTS FOR FILE NAMES

Similar to folder names and structures, filenames must be:

- unique
- indicative of what the file contains
- in line with how you or your business think about information
- scannable with the human eye according to how you (and in a business setting, other employees) find information
- naturally ordered alphabetically
- consistent

Let's go through all these requirements one by one to better understand what they mean and how they play out.

Watch:

"How to Name Files,"

part of the Get Organized Video Series,

at bit.ly/NamingFiles

Filenames Must Be Unique

It is absolutely crucial that filenames be unique, especially if you work in a collaborative environment, and especially if you frequently copy files to and from a server.

In collaborative environments, people often intentionally overwrite files—for example, if I'm working on an article with an editor, we will intentionally work off one single copy of the article that's kept on a shared server. After he makes his edits, he'll simply save over the old version. (Our process is in fact slightly more advanced than that. We use the Track Changes feature in Microsoft Word to review all changes made during editing before they are committed. Plus, I always keep original copies saved locally on my computer in case something goes wrong during editing. Still, the point here is that the working copy of the file is a single file, i.e., with no file versioning, that's saved in a shared location.)

I've also worked in environments where the shared servers were not reliable, so to prevent losing my work, I would drag the file to my desktop, work on it locally, and then drag it back onto the server when I was done, without ever changing the filenames.

On the other hand, there are many more times when we don't want to overwrite files unintentionally. For example, let's say I have a new invoice from Gray's Electronics named Graysinvoice.pdf, dated yesterday. I might stick it onto a server in the "Invoices" folder, and I might get a warning that a file by that name already exists. I might also assume that because the invoice came in yesterday, someone else put it there—but I just had the accounting department sign this invoice, so mine must be the most recent one and the old one is okay to overwrite. The whole thing falls to pieces when someone asks me later that day to pull up Gray's prior invoice, you know, the one from two months ago... the one with the same filename, which is now gone.

If you implement a really good folder structure, you'll already have in place one safety net for avoiding this problem because the folder wouldn't be called "Invoices"—it would be "1305_MAY_Invoices," or it would be nested within the May 2013 folder structure. Depending on the kind of work happening in this office, frequency of invoices, number of vendors and contractors, and so forth, you would have a folder system in place that would prevent overwriting.

But having clear, consistently designed, and unique filenames puts a second level of protection into place. So for example, if the convention were to always code the invoice with a six-digit date for when it was received (year-month-day, such that 130401 indicates April 1, 2013), and perhaps also to add a unique identifier for the project referenced or vendor name or some other data, it would then be much more difficult to for an error to occur with unintentional overwriting.

Filenames Must Be Indicative

It's seems silly to state that a file's name should indicate what it contains, but I've seen it go wrong plenty of times. Many people assume that when they nest a file within a folder, the folder takes care of the larger category name. They also falsely assume that contents of a file that are most relevant to them will be also be obvious and relevant to anyone else who needs to access the file.

Let's take the invoicing example again. Say the accounting department finds invoices in three ways: invoice number, tax ID, and the fiscal month in which it was paid. Accounting couldn't care less that it's "Gray's invoice."

I personally use two major identifiers for all my files: numerical dates and codes. In my personal life, I blog a couple times per month. All the text files and photos that I use on my blog are classified with a four-digit date (year-month) and the classifier "bg" for "blog." A photo of a market in Montreal taken during a trip in September 2010 is called 1009bg_montreal_market.jpg. The four-digit numerals work for my blog files because I only write on average four or five posts per month.

Sometimes, though, I'll have dozens of photos from a particular month. In that case, I either code them with a six-digit number, adding the day to the end, or I abbreviate some other signifier to save characters so I can add more descriptive text to the filenames. For example:

- 1009bg_mnrl_mrkt_peppers01.jpg
- 1009bg_mnrl_mrkt_peppers02.jpg

I know before I even open the files that these are both photos of peppers that I posted on my blog (bg), taken in September 2010 (1009), in Montreal (mnrl), at the market (mrkt).

Your signifiers can and should be whatever makes sense to you, your colleagues, your business, and what's inside the files. Airport codes, like LAX for Los Angeles and LHR for London Heathrow, might make sense. Categories of work, such as RPT for report and IMO for internal memo might do the trick. Maybe your files are schoolwork, in which case you could use the class code, such as BIO-214 or PSY-101 as part of the filename.

Filenames Must be In Line With Your Thought Processes

In deciding how your naming conventions will work, you need to know how you or your business remembers information. Using dates often kills two birds with one stone because if you code the file for when it occurred or was significant, that number in the filename gets you halfway to having unique names. I will never accidentally open pictures from my Montreal trip from 2006 when I really want the ones from 2010, even if I shot photos at markets both times.

I absolutely recommend including a date in your filenames. The only real question is, which date is most useful to you? The date an invoice was sent or processed, the date the work was completed, or when the contract was signed? In a business scenario, executives, team leaders, and department managers should have final say, but the people who do the most day-to-day work should absolutely weigh in. They're the ones who will know what really makes sense.

Filenames Should be Scannable With the Human Eye

When you open a folder, you want to know its contents immediately, without opening files or squinting at thumbnail views. Devising the right file-naming convention includes figuring out what the key information is in each document.

I cringe when I see a file called resume.doc. Which resume is it? When was it updated? Is it a long version or a short one? Where will it be sent? Has it already been sent somewhere?

Here's a better filename: 1102_CV_marketing_digital.doc. That file might be the resume that highlights your digital marketing experience, whereas 1102_CV_short.doc might be the generic professional CV you have on hand for a recruiter. Just think of how much more productive you could be if you knew with high certainty what each file contained before you opened it.

Filenames Should be Naturally Ordered

Another reason I like to use dates as identifiers is because everything falls into chronological order when the folder is sorted by filename, which is the default. Sorting by actual file date only tells you when files were last updated, and that's unlikely to be the primary thing you want or need to know. If you always put the year-month-date at the beginning of the filename, you will always have order.

Filenames Should be Consistent

When you eventually do find a system you can live with, stick to it! Your file-naming convention should be just that: a convention. It should be a short list of rules that you follow. Once you have a good one in place, you might jot it down on a note and stick it in a place where you can see it until you've adopted the file-naming system as a habit. If you're consistent, you'll find you won't need the sticky note after only a few days. Coming up with the right filename will be second nature.

The payoff of having a clear and consistent file-naming convention may not be obvious at first, but it becomes extremely evident with time.

II. DEALING WITH OLDER FILES AND ARCHIVES

No one expects you to reorganize and rename your entire archive of data. It's not a valuable way to spend your time, and it's ludicrous to think that you could even pull it off. So what should you do with all those disorganized files and folders from the past?

For starters, you should not rename them. There's absolutely no need. It's a waste of time. The easiest way to tackle your archives—which does not include your current working files—is to break them into smaller parts and move them out of the way.

The easiest way to tackle your archives—which does not include your current working files—is to break them into smaller parts and move them out of the way.

So think about all your old files in two groups: old and really old. How you define old and really old is up to you.

For me, "really old" means I am at least 99 percent sure that

I will not access the file ever again—but it could happen. It also should be at least three years old. Files that meet those two criteria are ready to archive to disc or an external hard drive.

Regular "old" generally refers to files that I worked on between one and three years ago. These stay on my hard drive or server where I can access them if I need to, but get dumped into year folders (see Chapter 1). I have folders for 2012, 2011, and 2010.

If your "really old" stuff doesn't take up that much space, you might just treat it the same as "old" files. Keep them hanging around nearby, but sweep them into year folders.

Putting older content into folders by year lets you do a spring cleaning. Have you ever tried to thoroughly clean your closet without emptying it first? It doesn't work. To get organized, you need a fresh start. Sweeping all your files into folders by year gives you that clean start without removing anything you might actually need. You need to see a clean and tidy window before you can get organized.

What do you do with a file that spans multiple years? Stick it in the most recent year folder. Did you work on it last year? Then drop it in last year's folder. If you're worried you won't be able to find it, why? Your files are already a mess! The point is to not overcomplicate this project of dealing with your archives. They don't have to be perfect, but they do need to be dealt with.

It's hard to give yourself a fresh start if you're staring at a pile of junk from years ago. Get it out of sight so you can move forward, and don't worry about renaming all those old files.

In my heart of hearts, I would recommend deleting files you don't need anymore. Just let them go. But realistically I know it's hard to do. So if you're in that camp of people who have a hard time deleting anything, keep your files but physically move them off your computer. It's very unlikely you'll ever look at them again, but you'll have peace of mind knowing they aren't gone for good.

I archive my "really old" files to disc because I simply don't need them eating up space on my local machine. They're also backed up in a cloud service (see Chapter 6).

What should you do if you keep files that you know you simply don't need anymore, but you just can't let go? Put simply, you need to move them or delete them, and it's much more of a psychological problem than a digital organization one. See the Additional Content at the end of this chapter for more on why learning to delete is crucial.

III. BUSINESS: SMARTER FILE SHARING

Communication is the lifeblood of every business. Yet too many business leaders, caught up in day-to-day challenges, overlook the need for giving employees practical ways to share information. In my mind, encouraging collaboration and information-sharing needs to be both part of the corporate culture and part of the daily processes.

What I mean by "information-sharing" encompasses oral communication, written documentation, maintaining a server, written email, and more. For the purpose of this chapter, I'll focus on electronic documents, but it's extremely important to consider how information-sharing happens across the organization and at all levels.

The Importance of Sharing

Businesses that share information effectively also have effective operations. Giving employees the information they need to succeed at their jobs and do them better increases their job satisfaction, too.

When information is not shared well, businesses run less efficiently and waste money. Every time a new employee joins the team—whether as a permanent replacement, temp (disability, maternity leave, sabbatical), or in a new role—that person needs to learn a huge amount about his or her job function, as well as how the business operates. When employees share information well, new team members learn what they need to know faster. And what they really need to know is how and where to find information, rather than specific answers to questions. It's the "teach a man to fish" principle.

One of the most expensive costs in a business is hiring, because of the time lost in getting new employees up to speed. The quicker employees figure out how to answer their own questions, the sooner they can make significant contributions. A business' goal in improving information-sharing across the company is to make it easy for people to solve their own problems. Another goal is to minimize the number of times people repeat the same mistakes. Imagine how much more smoothly and profitably a business could operate if it minimized these costs.

Types of Information Employees Share

Let's consider a few specific types of information that should be shared: procedural documentation, staff organization charts, workflow charts, staff contact information, client contact information, and human resources forms. In all likelihood, your business has made HR forms easily accessible to all employees, usually because the law requires it. When it comes to all those other documents, though, chances are they're out of date or they don't exist at all.

A lot of the information that should be written down is stored in someone's head, and that's problematic for a number of reasons. For starters, one person should never be the sole keeper of any business-critical information. It's just too risky. If that person falls ill, leaves the organization, or comes to resent people or practices within the organization, it could set the business back years! Second, when information is stored in someone's head rather than in a visible location, no one else can contribute to it. Third, other people who need the information are never sure if they have the most updated version. The reasons go on and on.

One of the most amazing assets of today's entry-level workforce is that they know how to look stuff up. If they need to know something (such as how to write formulas in Excel) and can figure out the basic terms used to describe it, they can find the answer online. All too often, businesses are not designed to support this kind of self-sufficiency. In the workplace, you can't always look up the answer. Sometimes you have to hunt down people and shake information out of them. The answers aren't stored in a searchable place, although they should be. A little bit of effort in organizing what should be shared can go a long way.

4 Steps to Start Sharing

Here's how you break down an information-sharing project into four steps:

- Explain the importance of sharing. Bluntly tell the people in your organization, in a 15-minute meeting, why having shared documents is crucial to the business.
- Set aside some time to update existing documents or have someone write a fresh document. These documents should comprise procedural manuals, documentation, and workflow charts. If your business is arranged into teams, each team should meet to discuss what documents they need to assemble or update. They can also prioritize which documents are most important to create based on what knowledge lives only in one person's head.
- Give each team half a day to write or update their documents. If you don't provide adequate time, the project will get pushed off indefinitely. The goal of the project is to set up the documents the business

needs—not necessarily finish every one entirely that day. These should be living documents that are updated frequently, at least once a year.

• Move the documentation to a shared location where everyone can access it, such as a folder on a server with the word "Documentation" or "Resources" in it. Do not relegate these documents to email. They must live in a location where everyone can access them and which prevents multiple copies from circulating. They're meant to be living documents.

That last step is crucial and deserves a word or two of explanation.

Living Documents

A living document is one that changes with time and typically can be changed by a group of people, not just one administrator. It's crucial that everyone who is affected by the documents has a chance to weigh in on how they're handled and what's in them—even junior staff, who might in fact be the most knowledgeable people about certain tasks.

The whole purpose of living documents is to make them open and transparent to all the people who need access to them, both now and in the future.

A friend of mine at a nonprofit spotted an error in spreadsheet that his organization had been using to calculate costs in a department. The spreadsheet contained incorrect formulas, and the person who had set it up had locked the file—and retired a few years earlier. After a little poking around on a shared server, my friend found a document that only senior staff could access, which contained the password. He was extremely lucky that the previous employee had thought ahead to put that information in a place where the right people could find it. Even in this case, however, it would have been better had my friend (and all the senior staff) known ahead of time that this document with the password existed, where it was located, and what it was named.

Consistency

Living documents can be kept on shared servers, but even then, you'll need to roll out guidelines for naming conventions so that as people add new files and folders to the server (or archive older files), they do it in a consistent manner. If everyone is on the same page, the names will be consistent, and everyone will be able to find what they need quickly.

IV. TAKE-AWAYS

- The file-naming convention you use needs to be something you understand rather intuitively, or in a business, something everyone in the organization can understand. It must have logic behind it.
- File-naming conventions should help people find information quickly by scanning names or by looking for dates or other signifiers in the name.
- Files that are "naturally ordered" are easier to scan and sort.
- Be consistent with how you name your files. It's more important to have a system in place moving forward than it is to go back through your archives and rename all your files from the past.
- Avoid a huge overhaul project by simply archiving older data by year, rather than renaming it.

- Sharing information is crucial to business success and requires everyone's participation.
- Living documents can and should change over time. They must also be accessible to multiple people who are able to change them, as well as visible to all the people who rely on them, both now and in the future.
- Documents that are labeled and stored in a consistent manner are easy to find, and thus will actually be used.

-

───────────

- Additional Content -

Let It Go: Why Learning to Delete is Crucial

Learning to delete files, emails, and other data is crucial to becoming more organized. Just because you don't pay any more, monetarily speaking, to keep another gigabyte or two of data on your machine, doesn't mean there isn't a cost.

Keeping information in our line of sight that we simply do not need creates "noise," as it were. This noise is distracting. It prevents people from being able to focus on what's most important.

If you've ever found yourself unable to delete messages from your email inbox or files on your computer because you "should" do something with them, even though you haven't yet and probably never will, I want you to try a sweeping exercise. Create a folder on your local computer (or in your email—wherever you are keeping data for no real reason) and label it "Later." Sweep all the email messages or files you know you don't really need but can't seem to delete into that folder.

Bear in mind, you're not deleting anything. You're simply moving it into a new folder.

Now just wait. After a few days, ask yourself if you ever once had to go into that folder to find anything.

Let it sit a while longer, maybe a month or two. Did you ever once even go hunting in that folder? If the answer is no, you have proved to yourself that you really do know what kinds of data can be deleted, archived, or at the very least just set aside away from the information that's most important to you right now.

II

Part II: Online

4

Email

Many of us have a love-hate relationship with email. Email can be at once a saving grace and your worst nightmare. On one hand, it lets you communicate with practically anyone in the world at a very low cost. It also gives you the flexibility to respond to messages in your own time, or asynchronously, unlike telephone conversations, which are by their nature synchronous forms of communication. Email creates an undeniable record of conversations, complete with time and date stamps. Sometimes it works as a backup system: "Where on earth did I put that file? Well, there's probably a copy of it in my sent mail folder at the very least." We cultivate social lives through email, keep track of work, and get coupons and deals sent directly to us without ever generating a single scrap of paper junk mail. What's not to love?

On the other hand, email has this uncanny ability to stir a cauldron of frustration and loathing that bubbles deep within us. The ever-growing number in bold and in parentheses indicating an absurd amount of unread mail in our email programs can make us feel like failures. We may have every intention of processing all that unread mail, but it feels impossible to do when the incoming messages never stop. So we perform a bit of triage, trimming the weeds as it were, but never fully yanking out the root. Even when messages aren't strictly work-related, they often still feel like responsibilities. I can't tell you how many times I've looked at my inbox, seen three unread Dictionary.com Spanish Word of the Day emails, and felt sheer guilt for not having read them.

This chapter aims to give you a comprehensive system for dealing with your email permanently. I'm not one for short-term solutions, and getting a grip on email isn't totally easy, although I think you'll find that some of my suggestions will make you feel like you're making a lot of progress early on, which in itself can be a motivating factor for sticking with the program in the long term. As with folder management and file-naming conventions, email management requires a lifestyle solution. You need to develop rules and principles that you can live with every day. Remember that staying organized is similar to maintaining a diet and exercise regimen. Not doing so and treating organization like it's a one-day spring-cleaning job is similar to going on a crash diet. Any results you do see will be very short-lived.

So before you dive into your email reorganization project, take a moment to recognize that you don't have to be perfect. The goal is to come up with rules for living that you can reasonably stick to and that make your work or personal life easier, more efficient, more productive, and better. If two weeks from now you're fretting the fact that you messed up and didn't follow your own system for a day or two and fear that renewed chaos is just around the corner, then your system isn't working. It needs to be forgiving of bad days. It needs flexibility built in. Sure, the more consecutive bad days you have, the harder it will be to recuperate (remember the dieting analogy), but one or two bad days shouldn't blindside you. My suggestions for organizing your email accounts take all these points into consideration.

I. HOW TO MANAGE EMAIL...IN THEORY

The whole trick to managing email is efficiency.

Figuring out what is efficient and implementing rules that steer you toward those efficiencies so you can develop habits in which you carry them out is not easy.

Let me back up, break it down, and explain it slowly.

Efficiency

Efficiency in email means not wasting your time. Because of how we use email—and sometimes because of the way an email program is designed—many of us have a tendency to waste time while using it. Microsoft Outlook, a true beast among software, works as the perfect example. Outlook includes so many buttons and features, from scheduling to task management, that it's easy to get caught up configuring one tiny piece of it without even knowing whether that configuration (which of course takes hours to figure out how to do) will have any significant payoff. For example, once a year, I have to dig through some help files and re-learn how to set up my out-of-office message so that it sends a custom response to contacts outside of my company but only alerts coworkers within the company once. Paradoxically, I end up sifting through my work email every few days while I'm on vacation anyhow just to stay on top of it. Setting up an out-of-office reply was likely a complete waste of time in the first place, but because the feature exists, I almost feel like I'm expected to use it.

Another way people tend to be inefficient with email is in how they reply, which is to say they write more than is necessary. Writing well and clearly takes skill, practice, focus, and self-awareness. It's not easy. So much of our efficiency with email hinges on writing, though. An email that's unnecessarily long doesn't just waste the writer's time to compose. It also wastes the reader's time. Keep it tight.

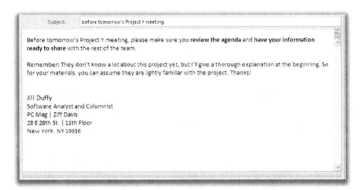

Figure 4-1: Short emails help everyone cut down on email inefficiencies.
Write tight as much as possible, but never at the sake of clarity.

All too often, I see back-and-forth email exchanges between people trying to chisel away at the meaning of a message that's shrouded in unnecessary verbiage. There comes a time when picking up the phone or walking over to someone's desk and speaking with him or her directly clarifies the matter quicker and more efficiently than hashing it out over email. Yes, sure, we all ought to be clear in what we write, but people who lack strong writing skills sometimes aim for clarity through length, which often creates more confusion, not less. Don't get me wrong. There are times when it pays to take your time writing a long email, making sure you nail down every detail, such as when you write an email that will serve as a document for others, say, the specs of a new project or summary notes from a meeting. But you have to consider that payoff and not waste your time and the recipients' time by writing too much when it isn't there.

Rules

All organization really boils down to rules. If you want to have an organized closet, for instance, you have to set rules for yourself about how you hang your clothes and where to put your shoes each and every time you take them off. Keeping an organized computer, as I outlined in detail in Part I of this book, really comes down to creating a series of rules for how you'll name files and where you'll put them. It doesn't matter if those files are PDF invoices, or photos of grandchildren, or recipes.

A lot of the "rules" I suggest for managing email closely mimic the rules I use in computer file and folder management. Email, however, has a whole other element: incoming mail, which is to say, new files that you didn't necessarily ask to receive. So you need a new set of rules for dealing with the bombardment of stuff that other people throw at you.

Habits

The lynchpin that holds rules and order together is habits. Habits are how you do the rules. If the rule is empty the email trash at the end of the day, the habit is always right-clicking to dump the trash before you quit the email program. If the rule is to always answer an email from your boss by day's end, the habit might be automatically sorting messages from your boss into a special folder and checking that folder every day at 4:00 p.m.

I like to use words like "habits" and "routines" to describe what I will do to stay organized because it creates more self-awareness about what it is I'm trying to do. For example, I'm not really trying to respond to my boss's messages once a day. What I'm really trying to do is create a habit that doesn't let me forget to answer his emails. The difference is more than semantics.

Managing email well and efficiently is about the system you use, not the software you use. Apps, features, and plug-ins may help solve specific problems you have, but if they are not comprised by a more comprehensive system of rules or method for ingraining habits, they won't come with long-term payoff. They'll act more like dieting pills than a lifestyle change. Occasionally I think an app, service, plug-in, or other third-party "solution" for email management can work as a motivator, the same way buying new sneakers might motivate you to go back to the gym. Motivators like those, however, only work for a limited amount of time. If the motivator doesn't get you to develop some deeper and more meaningful habits, then it was only a short-term solution.

II. HOW TO MANAGE EMAIL IN PRACTICE

Just as the computer desktop is an area of focus (see Chapter 1), your inbox is an area of focus for email. It's like a home page, or a landing page. It's where you navigate to reorient yourself after you complete a task and are ready to move onto the next task. So the first step to better managing email is to reclaim your inbox.

Step 1: Reclaim Your Inbox

For greatest efficiency, the inbox should be a clean and sparse place. If your inbox makes you feel like you're drowning, that's a problem. Here's how to get your head above water quickly so you can move onto other aspects of organizing your email system: sweep your inbox.

If you read Chapter 1, you already know that "sweeping" basically just means reclaiming your area of focus by moving a whole bunch of clutter to another location so that it's out of the way. You could theoretically set aside a few hours to thoroughly clean your inbox by actually processing the mail that's inside, but let me assure you that doing a sweep will be more efficient. For one thing, it will let you quickly move on to some of the other email management methods that you should start doing sooner rather than later. It will also help you start to develop habits of efficiency. Forget about processing every message. It isn't going to happen, and there won't be any big payoff. Doing a sweep is better.

Here's how I would do it (this will sound eerily similar to Chapter 1:

- Set up a few new folders in your email program and name them years, such as 2010, 2011, or 2012, or by quarter if you work on a quarterly calendar. Do not make a folder for the current year.
- Sort or perform a search, depending on which email program you use, to isolate all the messages from a particular year, and move them en masse to the corresponding folder.
- Whatever is left in your inbox—those are the messages you can actually worry about processing, maybe today, maybe tomorrow, but more likely, it'll be little by little over the next couple of days. You don't want to take on too much at once.

If your current year's worth of emails still feels overwhelming, you could repeat the sweep with month folders starting with January until what's left seems reasonable to you. The exact number of emails that constitutes a reasonable amount depends on context and personal preference. Personally, I couldn't tackle an inbox that had more than about 300 emails, but the number that seems reasonable to you could be significantly higher or lower.

Part of the underlying concept of the sweep has to do with preservation. You're not deleting or archiving any messages. You're not making piles that will be any harder to sift through later. You're just putting messages into buckets to break down one enormous task into more manageable parts. And in fact, there's more bucketing to come.

Step 2: Compartmentalize

Notice how the "sweep" only takes care of message you already have. It doesn't do anything for the messages that will be rolling in any second now. So once you have an inbox that doesn't feel suffocating, you can start to compartmentalize going forward.

I compartmentalize my email on two levels.

First, I have four different email accounts: one for business, one for personal communication, one for online shopping (where I keep receipts, track packages, and get banking and electronic tax filing alerts), and one for what I call "junk." My junk account isn't actually for junk in the strictest sense. It's related to an address that I use to sign up for newsletters or new online services that I want to try but that which are ultimately not important. Nothing that is mission-critical will ever go into that junk account, so if I don't check it for several days, it's no big deal. On the other hand, knowing that nothing of importance will ever fall into that account completely frees me from worrying about it. I've never lost a personal email from a friend beneath two pages of travel reward program surveys because those two kinds of messages are completely separate from one another. I should note that I created this system long before email programs were any good at helping users deal with graymail (mail that isn't spam and isn't important, but lies somewhere in the gray area between those two extremes—for more on this, check out the Additional Content at the end of this chapter), or before they offered sophisticated sorting tools. Outlook.com is particularly capable of managing and auto-sorting email. If I were building a new strategy from scratch, I might pare down my compartmentalization into only two accounts—personal and work—which is something to consider if you're creating a wholly new system.

Second, I compartmentalize with folders. In my personal, business, and shopping accounts, I have a system of folders in which I store messages (I don't even bother with it in my junk account; there's no payoff in having it). The folder structures vary based on the needs of each account and how I process messages that come into them.

Some people disagree with me about using folders to house email messages. It's particularly rampant among Gmail users, who prefer to either leave all their mail in the inbox or "archive" it, which in Gmail means stripping the message of all labels, including the inbox label. These users say they leverage the search function to find everything they need instead of a folder system. Need an email? Just search for it, simple as that. The problem with search, though, is that sometimes the thing you remember about an email is not in fact a word used in the message.

For example, let's say a PR professional sent me a press release about a new health app. I don't remember the person's name or the name of the app. When I'm digging up information from my email account about health apps, I search for "health" but I don't find this message. Why? The PR contact called it "mobile medical assistance" and never used the words "health" or "app."

Or what about a case in which I don't remember that an email exists? Let's say I got a message about biofuels, and I thought to myself, "If I have time, I might write an article about this next month." When next month comes and I have time, I am not going to remember that one of my potential stories was about biofuels. What I will remember is to look in a folder of ideas labeled "Ideas for Future Articles." I cannot rely on my memory alone.

What we see in our email programs and on our computers is important. What we see, from folder names to inbox messages, should act something like a second memory.

I'll share with you how I arrange my email folders, how I name them and such. It might not be exactly right for you, but seeing the logic behind it certainly will. My system is completely straightforward, but it has one benefit that might not be apparent. It easily lets me move/archive or delete messages that are quite old, which many of us must do when we need to reclaim space.

Currently, I have two blocks of folders. The first block comprises year folders with month subfolders. These have the exact same structure as my desktop folders on my computer. My work revolves around publishing dates, so all the emails about an article I plan to publish in September 2013 go into the folder called 1309_SEP.

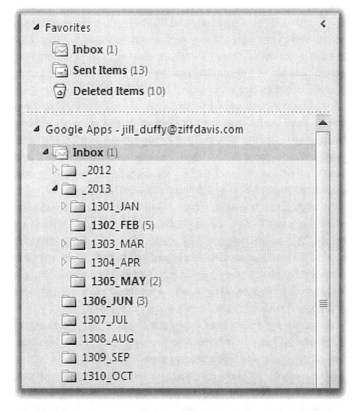

Figure 4-2: One way to manage email is to sort messages into folders, such as the ones shown here, to get mail out of your inbox.

If I have a special project or conference in a certain month, I sometimes make another subfolder within the month for messages pertaining to the event, but not always. It depends whether I will be receiving a lot of important messages from a number of different contacts for that event, such as a flight itinerary from a travel agent, a confirmation email from the event hosts, a few meeting requests from various executives, etc. On the other hand, if the event isn't too complicated, maybe because I'm only receiving emails from one person about it, then I know I can just sort by that person's name within the month folder to find everything I need.

The second block of folders I alluded to earlier in this chapter. They have to do with ideas, things I won't remember to search out but need a visual cue to help me remember. These folders have names that relate to themes, like Get Organized (the weekly series I write that resulted in this book), Health, Language Learning, Productivity, and so forth. All interesting emails about those topics that I might want to skim through at some point go into the appropriate folder.

Step 3. Review Your Options: FART

Have you ever heard about "farting" your way to better email? A woman once mentioned it to me after I gave a talk about email—I can't take credit for coming up with the acronym. I love that it's memorable, though. FART stands for the four actions you can do with an email message: file, archive, respond/resolve, or trash. Here's a little more explanation about what each of those options entails:

F: You can file messages into a folder to process later. "File" implies you will do something with the message later, perhaps read it or respond to it.

A: You can archive them, which may amount to nothing more than filing a message into a folder but saving it for reference in case you need it. Archiving implies you probably won't do something with the message later.

R: Responding to a message or resolving it means you do something with the message now, which might be replying with another message or completing a task that's assigned to you via the message. In other words, you do whatever follow-up action is necessary.

T: Or you can trash a message and call it a day.

In his book *Getting Things Done*, David Allen refers to a slightly different list of four actions that you can do with an email message: do it, defer it, delegate it, delete it.

Why do you need to remember FART? Well, you need to know what your options are before you can move onto the next step, which is developing a system for how to process email so that you don't have a long list of messages piling up in your inbox.

Typically, we receive two kinds email: action messages and information messages.

Information emails are the ones we almost always archive. They are messages you know you will need later for reference, but they don't require any immediate action or follow-up. They might include memos from human resources or party invitations from friends. You can file them locally, or you can export them to another system, such as Evernote or Microsoft OneNote. It doesn't matter where you put them as long as you know how to find them later and don't leave them piling up in the inbox.

Action emails usually require the "F" or "R" actions. Filing an email is not quite the same as archiving it. Archiving an email means you're done with it but don't want to delete it. Filing it means you need to return to it to do an action (which might simply be "read it"), but don't have time for it now. A lot of people don't file email—they leave everything in the inbox. If your inbox functions as your to-do list, that's likely the source of your pain.

Let me admit that although I file away a significant number of emails month to month, I do leave maybe two dozen messages in my inbox at all times. The messages in the inbox are usually ones that I plan to resolve next, while I file the ones I might put off for another few days or weeks. You don't need to reach true "Inbox Zero," a term coined by Merlin Mann that means having zero messages in your inbox, to be working with emails effectively and efficiently. Keeping a few messages in your inbox is totally fine. You just don't want to see an overwhelming number or a buildup of unimportant messages.

Trashing emails is something I do a lot (explained in detail in section IV of this chapter). For me, deleting emails is an act of letting go of the responsibilities they represent. Email messages often feel like responsibilities, even when they're not, and deleting them lets me free myself of that unintended negativity.

Step 4: Develop a System, Then Turn It Into a Habit

With a manageable inbox and basic structure in place for filing email, you now need a system for how you will file your email—beyond the basic rule of "emails related to June 2013 articles go into the 1306_JUN folder." When will you put them there? How often will you look through them? What will you do with the messages prior to filing them?

The rules you create should be explicit. You should be able to articulate them. But they don't have to be perfect or absolute. It's okay if you stray from them from time to time. Remember, the idea is to create a system that is forgiving of a bad day here and there, one that lets you bounce back easily if you slip up. I don't hold myself to these standards precisely every moment of every day. That would be neurotic and counterproductive. But I do aim to hit them most days, and I try extra hard on Fridays so that I can be in a decent position after the weekend on Monday morning.

Section IV shows some of my rules to give you an idea of how it works, although there's one more step to go still.

Step 5: Unsubscribe and Clean Up Lists

The next way to right a tipping email ship is to unsubscribe from lists, newsletters, and notifications that you simply do not want to receive anymore—the stuff that has no value. These lists might include business mail, like a weekly report memo that has nothing to do with you or your job, but that for some reason you have always received. If you can cut off the source of the clutter, you should, but you will need to set aside a few minutes to find emails that fit this description and click all their unsubscribe links. It doesn't take long in most circumstances—probably ten minutes at most.

At work ask to be removed from group emails face-to-face. The more we rely on email, the more apt we are to forget that some problems are best handled with a brief conversation. This advice may sound crazy and low tech, but it can be extremely effective. If you're part of a regular group email (say, a daily report or weekly project check-in) and don't want to be anymore, have a conversation with the person who manages or initiates that email, preferably face-to-face, or over the phone if you must. When you have a conversation face-to-face, though, you become human again. You're a pleasant person with a reasonable and straightforward request. Plus, if there is a reason you're meant to receive the messages, the person will explain why you've been included, and why you might have to start paying attention to those messages after all.

Another option in Microsoft Outlook is that you can "unsubscribe" gracefully and without notice from a thread by simply "muting" a conversation, although that leaves you stuck if anyone reuses the same subject line at a later date, as it's the target for carrying out the operation. (In other words, when you mute a thread, Outlook automatically moves to the "Deleted Items" folder any messages containing the same subject line of the offending email.)

In my opinion, social networks handle opt-in messaging much better than email does. Take the case of my friend who was grousing about her book club. If the organizer had set up the next book club meeting invitation on Facebook rather than via email, getting the information would have felt less obligatory for the members. Facebook events are optional. You can get to them and digest the information when you feel like it. When the same event invitation arrives via email, reading it and all the follow-up emails feels mandatory.

BUSINESS: In businesses, alternative communication tools can also help cut down on unwanted emails tremendously. Instant messaging programs let colleagues talk when they have something to communicate quickly and want an equally quick response, and also don't need a paper trail. Business social networks generally have areas where people can discuss ideas that are off-topic from work.

Perhaps the most common solution for managing unwanted emails is to set up automated sorting rules, or filters as they're sometimes called, that put the unwanted messages into a designated place (usually a folder, but sometimes the trash) before they even hit your inbox. All the major email programs have this feature. Find the email you don't want anymore, identify something concrete and fixed about it (always the same keyword in the subject line, sender, etc.) and set up a rule that sorts all those messages into a new and appropriately labeled folder.

Bear in mind that using automated sorting effectively relies on creating a new behavior: checking the designated folders. If you forget that you set up the new sorting rules, you might find that, several days later, a stack of emails has piled up in them, and now you're basically back to the drawing board, only the overwhelming emails are in a new folder rather than your inbox. If you choose to use automated sorting, just be diligent about processing those sorted emails on a regular basis. I recommend creating no more than two or three folders for automated sorting.

Whatever organizational system you create for yourself or your business, focus on lifestyle-like habits and general rules. You don't have to be perfect every day. You just need to come up with a system that will keep you on track most of the time and let you recover quickly if you have a bad day or two or three.

III. EXAMPLE RULES AND HABITS FOR PROCESSING EMAIL

To give you an idea of how this all plays out, here are some of my rules for processing email. The rules you create for yourself need to take into consideration the kinds of emails you get, how many you receive in a day, what kinds of follow-up actions you might need to take regarding emails, how you should ideally process them, and so forth. It's very context-dependent, but I think seeing a few of my rules will help you make some sense of how to develop your own.

Rule 1: Delete Quickly

If an email doesn't require action, including rereading or archiving for reference, I throw it away immediately. I cultivate deleting messages quickly into a habit by deleting messages in bulk first thing every morning. When I arrive at my desk, I delete as many messages as I see fit in one fell swoop. It's usually about 60 percent of my new unread messages. A few hours later, I do another check in which I delete messages that don't require action again. Usually, I can tell by the subject line whether the message is ripe for deleting. If there's any doubt, though, I leave the message alone until it's time to start processing the inbox matter.

Rule 2: Respond to Critical Messages Immediately, or Keep Them in the Inbox

If an email is critical—meaning it requires imminent action or deep rereading and possibly a reply—I act on it immediately or leave it in the inbox until I can act upon it, usually within a day or two. It can stay in the inbox up to a month or so. After a month, I must act on it. That's the deadline. Once I've taken action, the email is filed to its corresponding folder. Too many of us have emails in our inboxes that we think we will process any day now, when really, the ship has sailed. If you have a message in your inbox dated four months ago, seriously ask yourself whether you will actually ever do anything with it. I almost always have two messages in my inbox that I know are fruitless to keep, and yet I hang onto them thinking that one day, something will change. It won't. (I'm working on it.) Be realistic and let them go. For me, the habit around this rule is to mentally let go of most things that aren't in the inbox anymore, but treat what is in the inbox as important.

Rule 3: File By End of Day

If the email contains information I need, but does not require immediate action, it should be moved to its corresponding folder by the end of the day, or the end of the week if I'm busy. If I'm afraid I will forget to act on it because it's not immediately visible in the inbox, I can create a calendar item as a reminder. The email must be filed in a folder.

Rule 4: Clean Out the Inbox Friday Afternoon

Friday afternoon, I give myself 10 to 20 minutes to sort through whatever is in the inbox and perhaps act on the items that don't require a lengthy response. By the time I leave the office, I should be able to see an inch or two of white space at the bottom (room to fill up again over the weekend). The habit I've developed around this rule is to make Friday afternoons pretty relaxing starting around 4:30. I chat with coworkers, turn back to my computer monitor, and process a few messages. I like that I can do this activity while I'm also socializing, and because I like it, it's an easy habit to keep.

Rule 5: Archive or Delete After a Year

After about a year, archive it or chuck it. I tend to keep email data for about a year and archive everything else, which is extremely easy to do when your information is sorted into folders by month and year. Seeing as this rule is an annual event, I don't really have a habit that accompanies it, although I typically do a big cleanup on my physical desk, computer desk, files, and so on sometime either just before or after the New Year, and I roll this process into my annual routine.

Rule 6: See the Bottom of the Inbox

Day to day, this rule is the one I live by at the most fundamental level: Always see the bottom of the inbox. Unlike Inbox Zero, I aim to have no more inbox messages than I can see on the screen. It's simple. It's forgiving. It's flexible. It's a reasonable and attainable goal. And it doesn't take much to follow this rule consistently. It plays out as a habit in that once I started aiming to see the bottom of my inbox, it became a subconscious goal. I'm so used to trying to reach a single page of inbox material that all the other habits support this rule. There isn't a single habit that goes with it.

IV. OTHER EMAIL MANAGEMENT TIPS

I want to share some of my personal favorite email tips. These are small habits that I've developed over the years and use every day, often multiple times a day. I've tried to explain them in a way that will apply to most people, but bear in mind that how you use email might differ from how I use it. And that's kind of the point. There are likely shortcuts and efficiencies that I've found because of the way my work flows—the types of emails I receive, the frequency with which I receive them, the kinds of actions I'm expected to do with an email, etc. But do look through my examples to see if your work and mine match at all. There may be some ideas you can borrow or adapt to fit your own unique situation.

1. Delete First

I've already mentioned this tip above, but it's crucial to how I process email. When I open my email inbox every day, the very first thing I do is delete unnecessary messages without even opening them. I do this step even before opening and reading high-priority mail. For these messages, I can tell from the subject line whether they require action—usually they don't. I once spent a couple of days paying close attention to what kinds of emails I delete offhand and how many they are. It's typically a combination of messages from coworkers saying, "I'll be out sick today," or, "I'm running late," and unsolicited PR emails that are misdirected, such as someone pitching me an article idea for a topic that isn't within the scope of the publication where I work. I found these kinds of messages accounted for about 60 to 70 percent of new unread mail. In other words, I delete more than half my new messages before I even start reading email.

Keep in mind that moving messages to the trash bin does not wipe them out immediately. If I realize later in the day that a message I threw away was in fact important, I can still retrieve it, so long as I haven't dumped the trash yet. For my business email, I only empty the trash once a day at the end of the day.

2. Write Short

There was a time when I was highly concerned with writing complete sentences, creating complex and varied sentence structures, and addressing my email recipients uniquely in all my emails. I wrote long and detailed messages. I used to write to a lot of professors (I edited academic journals for a time), and in that world at that time, formality and a showing of respect seemed to matter. And certainly, there are situations that call for adherence to formal language, and when the length of an email does in fact correlate to its level of detail. But nowadays, I'm of the mind that fragments can be extremely useful in the right context, and that many people in my circle don't care whether I address them as "Dr."

Yes, in some contexts, it pays to be highly detailed, to tease out precisely what you mean, and take advantage of the paper-trail aspect of email: There's a record of everything. But I find myself preferring concise language, so long as it's also clear and straightforward. Short sentences can get a message across just fine. So can fragments. Sometimes they're even clearer than long sentences.

The one major problem in trying to be terse is that the tone can be mistaken. To avoid sounding unfriendly, use "hedging words" to soften strong remarks. For example, instead of "These reports are wrong," try, "Could these reports be wrong?" or "I think these are the wrong reports."

3. Reuse Sent Messages

I have a couple of email messages that I send over and over again. One of them, just to give you an example, asks a group of managing editors whether they have any specific requests for content that I put into a weekly newsletter. I do not write this email week after week. Rather, I dip into my sent mail, retrieve the message from last week, hit "reply all," update the message as necessary (such as stripping out the "Re:" in the subject line), and resend it. Why do the same task over and over?

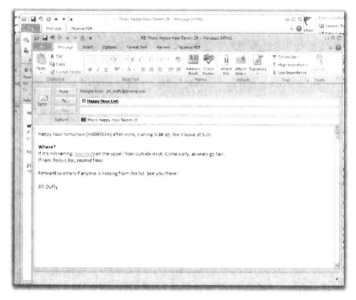

Figure 4-3: Reusing the content of old emails can help you reclaim time you might have otherwise spent writing the same message over and over again.

4. Sort to Delete

Data limits can sneak up on anyone, even highly organized people. When it's time to delete, I start by sorting my sent messages (in Microsoft Outlook) either by file size or attachment. Then I delete as many emails as it takes to free up space from the top two tiers of the sorting results (Outlook's two top tiers are "huge" and "very large"). The reason I delete sent mail before deleting messages from other folders is that I'm very likely to have a copy of any attachments I sent also saved locally. It's possible I want a record of having sent a file to someone on a specific date, but when I sort by file size or attachment in order to delete the largest messages,

I'm never looking at more than a dozen or so messages, so I can scan them and decide if there are any I'd rather keep. Still, I make big gains in deleting the handful of messages that I don't need that are huge.

Another group of messages to delete in a pinch is routine messages, in particular those that you have reused (see previous tip) or that have the same subject line (such as "running late"), or that are sent to one particular group. Sort your sent mail by subject or "To" field, and you can whack them to the trash in one shot. When sorting by subject line, keep the most recent two or three so you can continue reusing them.

5. Use Groups

I tend to email the same group of people repeatedly, so I set up Distribution Lists (that's what they're called in Outlook; they also called "groups" and "aliases"). Not only will you save yourself time by not having to type each person's name when you mail the group, you'll also set yourself up for easy deleting tactics, as I just explained in the previous tip.

6. Turn Off Notifications

I hate pop-up notifications of incoming mail. They're distracting. They also disrupt the habit I try to keep of only going into my inbox when I have a moment to process email. I don't want the email program to tell me when to do email. I want to do it when it's right for me based on other productivity tasks I'm trying to accomplish.

If instant alerts are pertinent to your job (and you'll know if they are), leave them alone. Everyone else: Turn them off.

7. Close Email to Focus

At work and when I'm trying to write at home, I'll often quit my email programs, including browsers for webmail, to focus. "Unthinkable!" you protest. Try it. It doesn't even have to be a long stretch of time. It can be 30 minutes. When email programs are open, it's tempting to check them periodically (or obsessively) for new mail. Quitting entirely removes the temptation.

V. TAKE-AWAYS

- Email is about efficiency. Focus on things that pay off.
- Having manageable email inboxes will make your work and personal life easier and better.
- In developing principles for handling email, cultivate lifestyle changes and daily habits so that you will actually implement the rules you create for yourself.
- Determine how you will handle email daily, weekly, and monthly, as well as how often you will archive email data. Remember to FART your emails.

VI. SUGGESTED TOOLS

- Evernote and the Evernote email plug-ins/Web clipper for Webmail is a note-taking and syncing program that can archive reference material out of email and into another system.
- Mailbox app (for iOS) uses the "snooze" function for emails, so they temporarily sift into another folder other than the inbox but reappear in the inbox as unread mail at a later date that you specify.

- Microsoft OneNote is another option for archiving reference material out of email into another system.
- Outlook.com is a useful webmail program because of its features for handling newsletters and subscription emails.
- SaneBox is a third-party email tool that automatically sorts messages from unknown addresses into a separate folder so that your inbox contains messages only from people with whom you've corresponded before.

- Additional Content -

Why You Should Have One Professional Email Address

When it comes to job interviews, anyone who has ever said that appearances make the first impression wasn't living in the era of email. The first thing hiring managers know about you these days is your email address. And they will make judgments, conscious and unconscious, based on it. Don't give them a reason to discard you too quickly. You need one email address that fits the following criteria:

- It must include your name in the address
- It must be hosted by a reputable, current, and known company: Gmail, Yahoo! Mail, Mac, Outlook.com are all fine
- It must not be a university .edu address
- It must not give away certain information about you (more on that below)

In a perfect world, your email address will be something like

NameSurname@host, but there are many variations you can try if your name is already in use by someone else. Some examples using the name Jennifer K. Gold are: JenniferGold, Jennifer.Gold, Jennifer-Gold, Jennifer_Gold, JenGold, Jen.Gold, Jen-Gold, Jen_Gold, JenniferKGold, JenKGold, JKGold, Gold.JenK, JK.Gold, etc.

Try different combinations using only elements of your name, and preferably the name people actually use for you (such as Jennifer, Jen, Jenny) before you give up. I highly recommend exhausting all these variations before you even think of including any other letters or numbers in your email address.

For your email provider, pick a current and reputable service. A free service works fine, as long as you use a known and current company. And while you might think using an .edu address makes a good impression ("I went to an Ivy League school!"), it allows recipients to question where you live and whether you've actually graduated. Those points are both very important when trying to get a job, so don't leave them in question.

If you *must* use an email address that is not your name, avoid these dead giveaways:

- a year, because people will assume it was the year you were born. Don't invite them to make assumptions about your age
- location, because people move
- hobbies or traits, again, to avoid discrimination
- anything off-color, to avoid insulting people or making yourself look foolish

When you're on the job market, you'll hear plenty of advice that boils down to "try to think from the hiring manager's perspective." The most important reason your email address needs to be your name is so that the very busy—and possibly highly disorganized—person who is screening applicants can find your email in his or her inbox quickly. A hiring manager will look for Jen Gold's email by scanning for J and G in the "address" and "from" field. Why? Because she might have 200 unopened messages in her inbox. She doesn't remember what day the resume arrived, and she didn't copy the files locally. That's how people operate when they're disorganized. They scan their inboxes for what they need. Even if the company has a Web form application system, there will still be a point when employers will connect with you via email. Make it easy for them to find you and your information by putting your name in the most important location.

\-

- Additional Content -

It's Not Important, But It's Also Not Spam: It's Graymail

The cashier at your favorite store offers 10 percent off, as well as exclusive discounts in the future, in exchange for your email address. Your friend recommends a daily deal newsletter that could help you save money if a bargain comes up that's right for you. These messages are graymail, solicited mail that you may want to read sometimes, but are never crucial. Graymail differs from spam in that the latter is unsolicited, whereas graymail comes at your request. Graymail can be a major source of clutter, especially if it goes unchecked for too long.

You could set up a separate email account for all your graymail. That's what I do. Then I'm assured my graymail will never be anywhere near my other emails. I don't even log into the graymail account (I call it my "junk account") unless I have time to browse newsletters, daily deals, listserv messages, and so forth.

Alternatively, you can use rules, filters, and folders to sort your graymail if you don't want to set up another Webmail account. For example, you might create a rule that says "if an email is from a sender whose address ends in 'nypl.org,' then automatically move the message to a folder called 'Library Notices' upon receipt."

How to Add Filters to Gmail: Tick the box to the left of whichever messages you want to filter, then select More > Filter messages like these. You can then apply the first set of rules to the filter, such as information about the sender, or the "to" name, or something in the subject line. Click "create filter" and you can apply the next step in the rule: what to do with the messages that meet the criteria (such as mark them as read, delete them, forward them to someone, etc.).

Note: In my experience, enabling rules in Gmail isn't always smooth. Links and buttons don't always work. Signing out and signing back in again seems to fix the unresponsiveness.

How to Add Filters to Yahoo! Mail: Tick the box next to any one message (no more than one or it won't work), then select Actions > Filter Emails Like These.

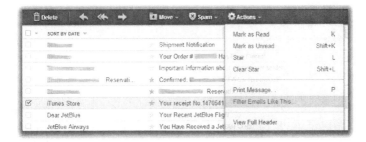

A pop-up box will let you fill out the rules for how to filter and sort similar messages.

How to Add Filters to Outlook.com: Outlook.com has many more included features for managing graymail. Microsoft's free webmail has a few ready-made rules that carry out some of the most common filters people want to apply to their inboxes.

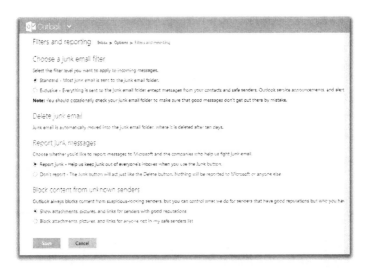

Much of the automation is managed through categories. For example, you can categorize a number of messages as "Newsletters" and then set a rule for what happens to all newsletters. Having categories makes it much easier to make changes to a rule later and have it apply to similar messages. You'll also find Unsubscribe and Schedule Cleanup options at the end of every message Microsoft knows to be graymail. Schedule Cleanup offers a few options for dumping messages from the same sender that may have piled up over time. My preferred selection is to keep only the most recent message from the sender, and doing so creates a rule to the same effect. When a new message arrives from this sender, any old ones will be deleted from the inbox.

The whole idea behind managing graymail is to keep those messages you may want to see sometimes separate from the messages you need to see as soon as they arrive in your inbox. Doing so will keep you happily reading updates from your favorite blogs, websites, news sources, social networks, and more, without hindering your ability to be productive and efficient the rest of the time.

5

Passwords

An absolutely essential component of digital life is how you go about protecting your online and connected identity. It almost always boils down to one thing that's in your control: passwords.

Think of how many passwords you have.

Actually, many of you probably have exactly three passwords: one for your bank and credit card logins that you think is especially strong, one for your email addresses, and one that's kind of weak that you use for everything else.

Am I right?

If I am, that's a big problem.

I. PASSWORDS: THE KEYS (PLURAL) TO YOUR DIGITAL LIFE

How Many Passwords Do You Have?

Think for a moment about how many logins you have. According to my password manager (a tool I fully explain in this chapter and recommend using), I have 181 logins, with new ones being added every month—181! "Sure," you're saying to yourself, "but you work in technology, so you have a whole lot more logins than an average person." Perhaps that's true, but I bet you have more than a dozen accounts that require logins. I bet I can even guess a bunch of them. Ready?

- home computer login

- work computer login
- smartphone lock screen (PIN)
- primary email account
- secondary email account
- bank account
- ATM (PIN)
- credit card account
- health insurance provider or benefits provider site
- home Wi-Fi password

Not convinced? I have more:

- Facebook
- iTunes
- Amazon
- eBay
- Netflix

You want more? I'm just getting started: LinkedIn, Twitter, Pinterest, The New York Times online, Instagram, Groupon, Orbitz, OpenTable, American Airlines, PayPal...

You get the point. Most of us have many more logins than we realize, and it's really hard to keep all those accounts totally safe without some help.

Copies of Keys

Passwords are the keys to your digital life. I think some technology writers overcomplicate the way in which they talk about passwords, so let me keep it simple with an analogy.

Think about all the physical keys you use. You probably have a house key, or maybe two house keys if you live in an apartment building: one for the building's front door and one for your apartment. You probably also have different keys for your car (I don't have a car, but I have two keys for my bicycle locks), your office, and maybe a mailbox.

All these physical keys are different. You don't have one key that unlocks everything, as it would be completely unsafe. Some keys you need to duplicate and share, like house keys, so that everyone in your home can get in and out. Some keys you have no control over how many are duplicated, as in the case of an apartment building's front door. A lot of people need a copy of that key, from the tenants to the building owner to the mail carrier—which is precisely why you have a different, unique key to your apartment door.

Think of passwords like "digital keys." What a lot of people don't seem to realize is that certain passwords really aren't secure at all, and that reusing a password is similar to having the same lock for all your doors.

I used to moderate an online forum that required each user to create a username and password, as well as provide an email address. The site never made any claims that the account logins were secure or encrypted. I, as the moderator, from time to time had to help a user retrieve or reset a password. All the passwords, usernames, and email addresses were fully visible to me. Let me tell you, it wouldn't have been hard to take anyone's username and password and try logging in to their email account with it. And I bet I could have visited any number of password-protected sites like the ones I listed earlier, and have successfully logged in as that person using the very same username and password. Chances are, I could have "hacked" into a lot of accounts with very little effort.

I didn't, of course—let me be explicit about that! But I could have because I know full well that the majority of Internet users use one "key" for all their online "doors." It's a terrible idea. And it's supremely lazy.

Fix Your Passwords Fast

This chapter provides step-by-step instructions for digging your-self out of the password-reuse hole quickly. It also outlines two methods for creating stronger passwords that are unique for every account you have, without taxing your mental abilities to keep them all straight.

II. CLEAN UP YOUR PASSWORDS IN 10 TO 30 MINUTES

If you haven't changed the passwords on your most important accounts in a long time, take about 15 minutes to do it today, or right now, literally while you're reading this chapter if you're in front of a computer that has a secure online connection. (I don't recommend doing it if you're on a wireless cell phone network or public Wi-Fi, though.)

Step 1: Prioritize Your Passwords

To fix a bad password situation quickly, focus on your most important passwords, the ones that protect the most important data. We'll deal with the others later.

In other words, prioritize which passwords are most important to change. For me, there are nine:

1. Google/Gmail
2. Yahoo! Mail
3. Hotmail
4. work email
5. primary bank account/checking account
6. primary retirement account
7. investment account (I have a lot of banks)
8. primary credit card
9. secondary credit card

My banks and credit card accounts definitely need to be well protected, but my email accounts are just as crucial. Any time you forget a password online, it's typically your email address that's used to retrieve it. If someone can get into your primary email account, they can probably get into your banking accounts, especially if you have undeleted emails from the bank telling the perpetrator where you keep your money.

I recommend choosing no more than ten accounts to mark as high priority. Remember, part of being organized is not biting off more than you can chew. You want to keep this task doable and manageable. If I told you to change all your passwords today you'd never do it. If I recommend you change the passwords on only ten accounts and no more, well, you can do that. I know you can.

You can have a second-tier list of passwords to change later. But seriously: Don't try to tackle them all at once. It'll become confusing and messy.

Step 2: Choose Either 'Recipes' or a Password Manager

Before you start changing passwords, you need a method. Changing your passwords is not the kind of task you want to start without first having a plan because you will find yourself flailing about, forgetting where you were, what you've done so far, and which new passwords you've put in place. Like I said, it can get messy.

Option 1: Recipes. I love password recipes. They're super simple to remember, and easy to create.

A recipe means you have some kind of mnemonic device or algorithm that you can do in your head that generates a password. Preferably, it's based on a set of words or algorithm that only you can compute.

Here's an example. Take some meaningful sequence of words, like "In Xanadu did Kubla Khan" (the opening words of Coleridge's poem "Kubla Khan"), and use the first few letters from each word: InXadiKuKh. Add to it four digits based on the first four letters of the URL you're logging in to, where A=1, B=2, etc. For example, the login for Chase.com would be InXadiKuKh38119. That's already a strong password that's not too hard to remember, but we can go one step further. Add one more function to your formula, such as "all banking sites get an asterisk (*) between the letters and numbers, but email accounts use a close parenthesis ( )) in the same location and social media sites take a pound sign or hash (#)."

So now we have InXadiKuKh*38119 as a login for Chase bank but InXadiKuKh#6135 for Facebook. The recipe concept works on song lyrics, famous events (JFK1963), or even something personal to you (as long as someone else couldn't easily guess it, such as the initials of your children).

As an aside, Chase bank actually does not allow non-alphanumeric characters, so we'd have to nix the asterisk. From time to time, you'll find that certain sites actually require non-alphanumeric entries in the password, but others don't support them at all. And those restrictions could change at any time. Very good password managers take care of this kind of thing for you, which is another reason they are superior to using a homegrown recipe system.

Figure 5-1. LastPass, shown here on Android, is a password manager that helps create strong and unique passwords for all your online accounts.

Whatever the case, just make sure your recipe is something you will remember and no one else could reasonably guess. You can even write your recipe down on a note and keep it in your smartphone or wallet; as long as you don't label it "password recipe," it will be pretty tough for someone to figure out what it means. For example, if I had a note in my smartphone that read: "Strawberry Fields Forever; cap S & B, slangy end" you would never know that it was a password recipe for "StrawBerryFields4eva"—and even if you did, there's not enough information there to give it all away, yet it is enough to trigger my memory if I forget.

Recipes are a fine solution if you're paranoid about using a password manager, but password managers (the second solution) are way more efficient.

Option 2: Use a Password Manager. A password manager is a piece of software or an online service that keeps track of all your passwords for you—or at least as many as you want to input. I'll explain about that in a moment.

A password manager does a lot of the work of making passwords and remembering them for you. When you first start using a password manager, it detects whenever you log in to a site and offers to save your current password in its system. Most password managers will check whether that password is weak, and if it is, offer to change it right on the spot. Additionally, it gives you the option to either devise your own passwords or let the password manager generate them for you. It also fills them in for you the next time you arrive at the login page. The only password you need is the one that unlocks the password manager.

I use a password manager called Dashlane, but I'm a little extra paranoid about my bank accounts, so I intentionally do not store them there. Instead, I use a recipe that I keep in my head for those accounts, although I have a note on my smartphone that reminds me of the recipe without actually spelling out what it is. (For more advice on what kind of notes to keep on your smartphone, definitely read Chapter 9.) Part of my rationale for what to include and not include in my password manager has to do with my plan for passing on my passwords after I die, which I share in Chapter 15.

Some password managers are free or freemium, and some cost a couple of bucks to use, but all the ones suggested at the end of this chapter were vetted by colleagues of mine who are security experts. In other words, they're all secure. They keep your passwords encrypted, while also making sure you have strong passwords and are not reusing the same ones over and over.

It's a little tricky to explain how password managers work without seeing it for yourself, so check out the video that shows one password manager, Dashlane, in action.

Watch:

"How Password Managers Work,"

part of the Get Organized Video Series,

at bit.ly/PasswordManagers

Step 3: Change Your Top 10 Passwords

With either a recipe in place or a password manager in hand, you can now go about changing your passwords. I recommend jotting down the ordered list of sites where you'll be changing your passwords and checking them off one by one as you go through them. If you're interrupted, you'll be able to remember which ones you completed already.

If this step takes less than 15 minutes, you might as well check that the mailing address and email addresses are up to date for all these password-protected sites, too.

If you're feeling more ambitious and want to redo your entire password system, say, by adopting a password manager, give yourself at least an hour, but know that realistically, you'll be chasing down passwords for a couple of weeks. There are some sites you simply won't remember that you have until you hit the login page. That's okay. Password managers are designed for just such a multi-day project.

The best password managers show you a little report indicating how many passwords you've reused, as well as how many are weak as opposed to strong.

Figure 5-2. Dashlane, another great password manager, shows you how often you have reused a password as well as which passwords are weak. It can also generate new and stronger passwords for those sites that might otherwise be vulnerable to attacks.

Step 4: Re-authenticate Your Devices

Hopefully your smartphone is nearby, because you'll want to re-authenticate any accounts on it for which you allow your passwords to be stored, such as email. The same goes for other devices, whether they're tablets, laptops, or an Internet-enabled TV. How sucky would it be to fire up the TV with a bunch of friends to watch something on Netflix, Amazon, or HBO GO only to realize you have to log in to that account all over again?

III. RECOMMENDED PASSWORD MANAGERS

When you log in to a secure website, your password manager captures the username and password, and the next time you visit that same site, the password manager offers to fill in the saved credentials for you. That, at its most basic, is the function of a password manager. Web browsers and some operating systems offer that basic functionality, too, but they typically don't provide any further assistance for helping you make strong passwords or for flagging your attention when you reuse passwords across different sites. Good password managers, however, do just that.

What about sites that have something other than a simple username and password login? For example, one of my banks uses a numeric-only username coupled with a password, and then asks for a six-digit PIN on the following page. The best password managers handle that kind of stuff with ease. Here are a few that my security-expert colleagues have vetted and that I recommend based on their approval.

Dashlane. Dashlane, which is freemium, is the password manager I use. I must admit that the first two weeks or so that I used it, I frequently felt frustrated because Dashlane kept prompting me to do this or that at every turn. The constant calls to action go away with time, though, after you've updated some of your weaker passwords and given Dashlane permission to save more of them from other sites. Dashlane also saves other secure information for you, such as credit card details and your shipping address for when you make an online purchase, which it can auto-fill. It can also save a record of all the online shopping you do. It works on Mac, Windows, iOS, and Android.

Kaspersky Password Manager. Kaspersky Password Manager automatically captures application and website passwords, stores them securely, and replays them as needed. It integrates with many browsers and offers a USB-based portable edition. It can fill Web forms with personal data, though its data entry process could be better.

LastPass. LastPass manages your passwords thoroughly and flexibly, with features that go way, way beyond the competition's. There's a free version and a paid premium version that's pretty inexpensive, and which adds a number of advanced features including enhanced multifactor authentication and the ability to run on almost any mobile device. LastPass stores your encrypted data in the cloud, but it's a very, very secure cloud. You can read a little more on where passwords are stored exactly in the next section. LastPass works for passwords on locally running computer programs as well as applications and online accounts.

MyLOK Personal. MyLOK Personal stores your passwords and personal information in a smart card encrypted by an on-board crypto chip. If storing encrypted passwords in the cloud or even on the PC makes you nervous, this is the password manager for you. Similar to LastPass, MyLOK works on local programs as well as websites.

Norton Identity Safe. Norton Identity Safe manages your passwords and fills Web forms with personal data. It can sync data between multiple Macs and PCs; iOS and Android apps are also available.

RoboForm. RoboForm has two affiliated products: RoboForm Desktop and RoboForm Everywhere. The desktop piece handles standard password management tasks, for both online accounts and locally running programs, and other auto-complete information, such as credit card numbers and home address for online purchase—and it's probably the best product on the market for that part. Its one weakness is that it's limited to a single desktop... which is why you'll probably want to add to it RoboForm Everywhere. "Everywhere" is what you need if you want RoboForm to work on several different devices. It's kind of neat that you can pay for it once and install it on as many computers as you want. So, you install RoboForm Desktop on any number of PCs, but you have to maintain a single online collection of passwords and form-filling data with the Everywhere component. You can access the online data directly, but you don't get full control without installing the Desktop edition.

Where Are Your Passwords Stored, Really?

The storage location for your personal data varies with different password managers. For example, LastPass encrypts your data locally and stores the encrypted data online. You can access your passwords from any location by logging into the online password vault. RoboForm Everywhere syncs passwords between multiple instances of an affiliated desktop program, RoboForm Desktop, but also offers online access. Dashlane gives you a choice of either keeping the passwords strictly on your computer or syncing to the cloud so they're accessible on all your machines.

The Big Picture

The organization you do now should support more organization or some other activity later. Updating your passwords and moving to a system of using either recipes or a password manager is actually part of a bigger plan. In the short- to mid-term, you'll keep your accounts safe and decrease the chances of getting hacked or becoming the victim of identity fraud. In the longer term, you're setting up a framework for solutions to other problems, like how to get help managing your online accounts if you become incapacitated or when you eventually die. I explore those morbid realities in the last chapter of this book.

IV. CHANGE IS GOOD

One additional aspect of online passwords that I need to mention: Change is good.

Annual checklist: Update your most important online passwords once a year. Some technology experts recommend doing it more often than that, whereas other experts don't think change is necessary at all as long as you use strong and unique passwords on all your sites. I personally recommend updating your most important passwords, such as your email accounts, once a year. I think that's doable and helpful.

It's not the end of the world if you don't change your passwords that frequently or at all. In fact, it's much more important that you use unique and strong passwords (see the Additional Content at the end of this chapter to find out what makes a strong password). But I'm still of the mind that changing the most important ones is good practice. It basically protects you if you logged into an account somewhere that was unsecure or public, such as a friend's computer or while on a hotel lobby public Wi-Fi network, and either forgot to logout (or had some other unforeseen compromise). Let me share a story with an example.

One time, a friend and I were discussing Netflix, and she mentioned that she didn't have an account.

"But I thought you just said you watched that Netflix-exclusive show," I said, confused. "Did you illegally download it or something?"

"Oh no," she said. "What I mean is I don't pay for an account. My friend logged into her Netflix account on my computer a couple of months ago, and I just never logged her out."

That's all well and good when it happens with people you trust, but you never really know for sure that they won't accidentally mess up your account details or pass their laptop over to a less trustworthy friend. Your account details might contain credit card or bank account information, your address, or other sensitive information.

Changing passwords usually forces any devices that are currently logged into that account to log out and ask for re-authentication in the form of the new password.

V. TAKE-AWAYS

- Use unique passwords for every online account.
- Never reuse passwords.
- Create strong passwords (see the Additional Content at the end of the chapter) either through recipes or by using a password manager that generates them for you.
- Changing your most important passwords once a year may not be necessary, but it could help keep your accounts just a little more secure.

VI. Suggested Tools

- Dashlane
- Kaspersky Password Manager
- LastPass and LastPass Premium
- MyLOK Personal
- Norton Identity Safe
- RoboForm Desktop and RoboForm Everywhere

- Additional Content -

What Makes a Password Strong?

There are two primary sources of passwords: humans and computers. A human can come up with a "recipe" for a password or simply invent one, whereas a computer can generate something at random.

Computer-generated passwords from a password manager

(there are six recommended password managers in this chapter) are strong by design.

Passwords you make up yourself, on the other hand, aren't necessarily so secure, unless you know a few characteristics that will make them secure. Generally speaking, strong passwords

- are at least 12 characters long
- contain letters and numbers, as well as at least one special character (such as an asterisk) when supported
- don't use words found in dictionaries of any language (this is true for invented words if they are nothing more than two known words smacked together to make an unknown word, like computerbooger)
- combine uppercase and lower case letters
- are different from the username
- don't use specific personal information, such as date of birth or surname

It's much preferable to use computer-generated passwords, although not everyone is into that. If you are gung-ho on coming up with your own passwords without the help of an app, try to use a password recipe or passphrase instead, explained in this chapter.

6

Backup and Storage

Most of us know we should back up our computers, but we put off doing it because losing valuable data is a threat rather than an imminent danger. Plus, the project seems overwhelming.

You might be saying to yourself, "It's going to take hours! I don't know what my options are, or what I need to buy, much less how to actually do it."

There are more questions, too. How do you know your backup system is working? How easy or hard is it to get those backed-up copies of files if you ever need them? Is it safe to use an online backup program, or does putting data in the cloud necessarily put it at risk? (You'll find a whole lot of information about "the cloud" in the next chapter.)

If backing up your computer is a chore you've put off for too long, this chapter will speed you through some of the most time-consuming steps and hopefully convince you to back up at least part of your computer: the stuff that matters most to you.

Figuring out your entire backup strategy may seem like biting off more than you can chew, so in this chapter, I break it down into several steps and smaller projects. You should be able to do the first one in a single day.

This chapter refers only to desktop and laptop computers (or "personal computers," whether they're Windows PCs or Macs).

BUSINESS The contents of this chapter aren't intended to be used for businesses, which might need to comply with certain regulations or best practices that are well beyond my knowledge, such as backing up company email for legal reasons.

This chapter also doesn't look at backing up mobile devices, such as smartphones and tablets—that's covered in Chapter 10.

I. THE BACKUP PLAN

To get yourself organized and motivated, imagine that the most important files on your computer—whether emails or the video of your child's birth—is at risk right now. Imagine they'll be wiped out by the end of the day if you don't do something.

What's the number one rule of backing up? Redundancy, redundancy, redundancy. Maybe you've heard that joke before. It means that ideally, you should keep more than two copies of anything you back up. Having only one copy is asking for disaster. Having two copies is better, but not necessarily safe. Keeping three (or more) copies of your files is nearly foolproof.

My theory about disorganized people who are trying to become more organized (that's you) is this: It's better for them to take baby steps and actually do something of value than set an overly ambitious goal.

Even if you believe that backing up is a royal pain in the neck, which it certainly can be, the whole process is made much more achievable by breaking it down into a plan.

The plan that I set forward here is designed so that it's valuable to you even if all you do is the first step. Sure, you should try to get through as many steps as you can, but if all you can handle are the first one or two or three, then at least that's better than nothing.

Watch:

"How to Back Up Your Computer,"

part of the Get Organized Video Series
at bit.ly/BackUpComputer.

_____

Step 1: Back Up Your Most Important Data

Which computer files have the most value to you? That's where you should start.

For many people I would presume the most important files are:

- personal photos
- home videos
- music collection
- tax forms from e-filing
- other personal records that may be digitized (such as a home owner's title)

If you're not backing up your entire machine, just selected files, I recommend using a cloud-based file-syncing service and a USB flash drive or discs (I'll explore additional options in the next section). This combination is extremely inexpensive and takes mere minutes to use.

Start with a simple file-syncing service. Pick any service you like. Two of my favorites are Dropbox and SugarSync, but dozens more are available. Here are a number of them that rate highly in general, although you might want to read up on each one's special features and services before you pick one:

- Amazon Cloud Drive
- Box
- CX.com
- Dropbox
- Google Drive

- iDriveSync
- SafeSync for Home
- SugarSync

Surf on over to the file-syncing service website of your choice and sign up. All file-syncing services have some kind of "get started" literature or video. Read or watch it, and pay attention!

Syncing is not the same as making a one-time backup copy of your files. The most important thing to know about file syncing is that if you delete files from your PC, they will also be deleted from the file-syncing services. If, on the other hand, your hard drive flat-out dies or is destroyed (fire, flood, etc.), the latest copy of all the files will still be available to you via a file-syncing Web account.

Download the software to your computer and follow the instructions, which typically amount to either dragging files or folders into a new "synced" folder, or right-clicking folders on your machine that you want to sync. If you organized your computer according to Chapters 1-3, this part will be a breeze, as you'll already have folder structures that make sense.

With most providers, you'll get anywhere from around 2GB to 10GB free space, which is probably all the space you'll need if you're only backing up your most important files and not other data, such as your email or your PC's settings.

Setting up a file-syncing service should take less than 15 minutes, plus additional time for all the files to make their way to the cloud (though you can do other things while that's occurring in the background). A nice feature of file-syncing services is that you can install them on a bunch of different machines and have them all link to the same account. Go ahead and install the same service on all your laptops and desktop computers.

When it's all said and done, your files will be accessible to you from any nearly any Internet-connected device. If your laptop incinerates, the files will still be online, and you can download them as ZIP files to make a new copy on a new PC. Remember, though: If you move your files to the trash, they will also be deleted from the syncing service!

Your secondary backup set of files can be something simple, like saving your files to disc or a USB flash drive. Blank DVDs don't cost much, and you can buy them at most office supply stores. USB drives are equally easy to acquire. Pop one into your PC, drag the files you want to back up into the device's folder, and give it a few minutes to process. Voilà. Two backups done.

Tip: To see how much space you'll need from a USB drive or disc, collect all the files you're going to copy into a folder, right-click on it (or, on a Mac, hold Command and click), and select Properties (Windows) or Get Info (Mac). You'll then be able to see how many megabytes or gigabytes the files take up.

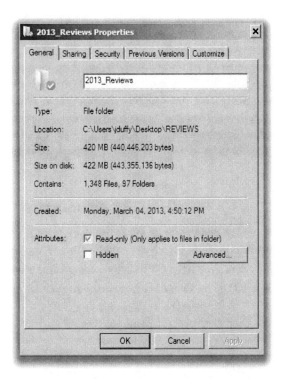

Figure 6-1: By right-clicking on a folder and choosing Properties, Windows will show the folder's size (420MB in this case). You'll need to know the size in order to pick a storage device that can hold one of your backups.

Backing up to disc or a USB flash drive works very well for files that you don't plan on changing, such as photos and tax returns. It's less effective for "working files" or files that are in progress and that you continue to edit—although file-syncing services are ideal for these. For example, I keep a master spreadsheet on my office computer that lists all the articles I'm writing, their state of progress, and whether I need to complete any precursor work prior to publishing them. I would be lost without this file. But it's a file that's actively being editing year-round, so if I save a copy to a disc or USB drive, I only have the file as it was saved at the time that I backed it up. So I keep this spreadsheet synced in my file-syncing program so that every time I change it, the latest version of the file automatically saves to the cloud as well as any machine where I have file syncing enabled.

What I do with files of this nature is sync them until the end of the year. Then in January, I transfer any remaining work to a new spreadsheet and rename it with the current year. All that remains on the original spreadsheet are articles that have published. The work is done. The spreadsheet becomes a record rather than an active file, and so I can back it up as if I were "archiving" it. (See the Additional Content at the end of this chapter.)

That's the quick and dirty way to back up selected files. At least you'll have covered your butt if you do that first step. Of course, I recommend putting into place a more thorough backup solution, which is what the next step covers.

Step 2: Back Up Your Entire PC

Different kinds of backup solutions work better for different kinds of data and your ability to retrieve them.

You can use a USB flash drive to back up your entire PC, which is surprisingly quick and simple, but you'd have buy a flash drive that has more space than your computer, and that gets pricey. Section III, which follows, looks at all the different options for where to back up your data and their relative costs.

As I mentioned, technology experts agree you should have more than two copies of all your data. You have the original set of data on your computer. That's the first one. Then you should have two backups, and those two should be in different physical locations. For example, if one of your backups resides on an external hard drive that you keep in your home—the same home where you keep your computer—your third backup has to be stored outside your home. The theory is if your home burns down, you'll have another backup copy that's safely kept somewhere else. Likewise, you wouldn't want to keep two copies of your data in two accounts with the same cloud service provider because it leaves you vulnerable if the company suffers an attack or some other disaster. Both sets of data would be at risk.

As I said, there are number of different ways to back up your computer. Pick two from the list, and devote an hour one weekend to configure them. You could finish in less time, but you'll have extra time in case you need to troubleshoot. Setting aside an adequate amount of time to do the job will help ensure you follow through with it.

Step 3: Archive Some Old Stuff

Continually backing up old data that you don't need just doesn't make sense. It wastes resources such as space and time.

Annual checklist: Annually, I like to archive to a more permanent backup device files that are roughly older than three years. It's a project I do around New Year's Day, sort of like an annual spring cleaning for my computer. I haul out the stuff I don't need any more and tidy up what's left. An equally good time to archive old stuff to get it off your computer is when you set up a backup solution.

If you followed the guidelines in Chapter 2 suggesting you divide your primary folders into year folders, figuring out what to archive will be a cinch. You could select files by hand and move them to the archival location of your choice, or you could set up folders by year now and work toward a larger picture of digital organization. Even if you plan to just archive a certain kind of data, like only photos, I still recommend grouping the files by year. All your files will be easier to find later if you ever need to pull them from the archives.

For my office work, I burn archives to DVD. I figure the company keeps at least one backup, and the DVDs give me a second way to back them wherein I also have quick access to the files, should I need them. None of my work is life-or-death crucial. If the building—and my computer, and the DVDs—went up in flames, it would be a shame, but it wouldn't be the end of the world. All the files I archive represent finished work, that is to say, articles that have been published, so I have a record of the finished published work as well (that's all online, and also backed up by the company). Although a super-duper secure person might say my archiving solution isn't ideal, I say it does what I need it to do. And that's what matters.

II. WHERE TO BACK UP YOUR COMPUTER: 7 OPTIONS

There are seven basic options for where you can back up your computer. I'll list them here in no particular order, and then explain what makes them different, as well as some of the pros and cons of each:

- the cloud (Internet-accessible storage, including file-syncing services)
- disc (CD, DVD, Blu-ray)
- USB flash drive
- external hard drive
- network-attached storage (also known as NAS or home server)
- another computer
- online backup service

1. Disc

Burning data to discs may sound out of fashion, but it's an inexpensive and reliable option for certain kinds of files, particularly original copies of photos and videos. It's also a good option for files and entire folders you want to archive and save, but rarely need to access, like PDFs of old tax returns. Retrieval is straightforward—pop in the disc, open the file.

One problem with discs is you will probably store them near your computer, so in the event of a physical disaster, they'll be subject to the same conditions, although you could tuck them into a safe or keep them at a family member's house, I suppose. They're portable, which sounds good at first but also means they're subject to being misplaced or damaged by other means. Discs also aren't ideal for files you need to change (anything in-progress, that is). And the biggest disc you can find will still fill up quickly with data.

2. USB Flash Drive

USB drives share many of the same benefits and disadvantages as discs: good for files and folders, inexpensive, it's fairly reliable, easy to retrieve information from them, and they're likely to be stored near your computer and thus subject to physical disasters. One noticeable difference: USB drives are a better option for storing active files because they're slightly more portable and typically a little better for read/write.

If you buy a large enough USB flash drive, you can use it to back up your entire machine. It's simpler than a lot of people realize. Just plug it in, and when prompted, choose the option to use the device for backup. Your PC should walk you through the rest in a few minutes.

3. External Hard Drive

External hard drives are big, offering a lot more storage capacity than USB keys and discs, and therefore are better for backing up the entire machine rather than just selected files. Like USB keys and discs, external hard drives are likely to be kept near your computer, especially because you have to physically connect them to your computer to use them. Most external hard drives are pretty rugged, though, and hence less likely to be scratched, cracked, or broken. Retrieval, again, is convenient.

External hard drives cost a bit more than the other options, but it's a one-time fee, unlike buying cloud-based storage, which will be billed as a subscription. Setting up an external hard drive takes only a few minutes. They're basically plug-and-play ready. You can makes copies of files to store as-is, or you can turn on the settings on your PC to back up files to the hard drive on a regular basis.

4. Network Attached Storage (NAS)

NAS devices are the next step up from external hard drives. They share many of the pros and cons of external hard drives, except they are often wireless and can be used easily by more than one computer at once. An entire household of users can back up their computers to a single NAS.

5. Another Computer

For people who use more than one PC, another method of backup is to simply store copies of all your data on both machines, similar to using an external hard drive or NAS. You can connect two computers with a cable or wirelessly by networking them. Again, if you store both PCs in the same place, they're both exposed to the same physical risks.

6. The Cloud

To be clear, by "the cloud" I'm referring here to services in which a company lets you upload copies of your data to its servers. But

I am not including specific online backup services (see the next entry for those). Here I'm talking about file-syncing services like Dropbox, Google Drive, and so forth, as well as slightly more specific cloud-syncing tools such as iCloud and Photo Stream (those are two of Apple's own cloud-based syncing and backup solutions for work files and photos, respectively).

Many services offer a good chunk of storage for free. Setup is quick (minutes). They're perfect for files you need to access regularly, as you can reach them from any Internet-connected device. And the data is hosted in a separate location from your PC, so if your house burns down with your laptop in it, your cloud-hosted files won't be affected.

The downsides: If you need to pay for extra storage, expect it to be a subscription fee rather than a one-time cost. You should also check that the service you choose is safe and encrypts your data. Plus, if the hosting company goes out of business, the destiny of your files isn't certain. Additionally, some of the services are very specialized and handle only music or only photos. Be sure you know exactly what the service backs up before you use it.

Some examples include Amazon Cloud Drive; Apple iCloud, Photo Stream, iTunes Match; Box; CX; Dropbox; IDriveSync; Microsoft SkyDrive; SafeSync for Home or SafeSync for Business; and SugarSync.

7. Online Backup Service

Finally, you can pay an online backup service to manage the whole kit and caboodle. The advantage is that specialty services are thorough, and they're physically separate from your computer because they keep your data in the cloud. Getting your data back may be trickier. It's in your best interest to test the process of retrieving your data before you sign up for a long-term subscription with any provider.

A few online backup services recommended by my colleagues

(who have more expertise and hands-on testing time with backup services than I do) are:

- Backblaze
- Bitcasa
- Carbonite
- CrashPlan
- IDrive
- Jungle Disk
- MiMedia
- Mozy
- Nomadesk
- Norton Online Backup
- SOS Online Backup
- SpiderOak.

Some online backup services are actually free for a limited amount of space (similar to file-syncing services), and the paid services can cost as little as $3 or $4 per month.

III. HOW TO BACK UP YOUR COMPUTER

To create backups of your data, you'll need some basic software. You can either use the program that comes included with your computer, or pay for specialty software, which tends to offer more options and features.

The best backup programs work quietly in the background, making copies of your files either on a regular schedule or whenever a new version of a file is saved to disk. There are two basic varieties of backup programs: file-and-folder backup software and disk-imaging programs. If you decide to make a complete backup (disk imaging), which doesn't take all that much more time than a partial backup, you'll still need to choose a type of storage, whether it's an external hard drive, or cloud storage space.

Solutions Included in Your Operating System

The "work" part of the backup can be done using Windows' built-in backup utility or Apple's Time Machine. Both come included with recent versions of Windows and Mac OS, respectively. You can set them to run as often as you like, and configuring them is relatively straightforward if you follow the wizard upon launching the program.

Backup software that you purchase will generally have many more options for letting you select exactly which files and data you want to back up, how you want to back them up, and to where. But the Windows and Mac tools work just fine.

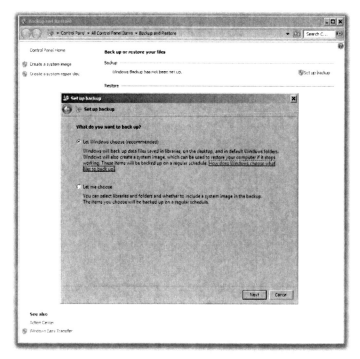

Figure 6-2: Windows' backup utility, which comes included on Windows computers (and is similar to Time Machine on Macs), has a fairly straightforward wizard for setting up backups.

If you're unsure what to use, I recommend exploring the included programs on your machine first. After you're comfortable with them, you might then look into other options.

File-and-Folder Backup Software

The file-and-folder backup programs protect only the files and folders that you specify, and typically give you the option to save the version history of certain files.

Backup software can, if you so choose, back up files to a different folder on the same hard drive that contains the original file—but that's all for naught is your hard drive fails. It's better to send files to a USB drive or a network location, which is why I didn't include the option to send to the hard drive in the list. Some can save to writable CDs or DVDs or even remote FTP sites. Some can create ZIP archives of your backed-up files, and some can save encrypted backups so that other users on your network won't be able to read your files.

The way these file-and-folder backup programs work is by asking you to select any folder or set of folders as a backup source. Some come with prebuilt backup strategies, such as asking if you want to back up your Windows desktop, all your webmail accounts and messages, or your Internet Explorer favorites. They're rigorous programs, costing anywhere from $30 to $75.

A few that my colleagues recommend are: Acronis Backup & Recovery, Genie Backup Manager, Paragon Backup & Recovery, and Rebit.

Drive-Imaging Software

Drive-imaging software backs up your entire hard drive. This backup is an "image" of the entire drive. Sure, you will have a more complete backup of your whole computer, but it's a little more difficult to retrieve files if you need them. If you need to recover a file, you have to use the software's file-retrieval function to grab an older version of a file from the image and copy it to your hard drive. That's the bad news.

The good news is that your image includes system files as well, so if your system ever becomes unusable, you simply run the drive-imaging program from a bootable emergency CD, and restore your entire drive, provided you stored it on a removable drive or NAS. If you need a new hard drive altogether, you simply install the blank drive, then restore your whole system from the backed-up image to the new drive. Drive-imaging programs require a lot of space for backups, because even a compressed image takes up almost as much space as the drive you back up.

Drive-imaging software costs roughly the same as file-and-folder backup solutions: in the neighborhood of $35 to $90.

A few that my colleagues recommend are: Acronis TrueImage, Norton Ghost, Paragon Hard Disk Manager Suite, and Shadow-Protect Desktop.

IV. TAKE-AWAYS

- If you don't have time to set up a thorough backup solution, at least back up your most important files.
- Back up your most important files using a simple solutions, such as
  - burning them to DVDs or CDs
  - saving them to a USB flash drive
  - syncing them to a file-syncing solutions.
- The best backup solution involves keeping at least three copies of your data in at least two different physical locations.
- DVDs and flash drives work well for archiving files that you likely don't need to edit.
- File-syncing services work well for making a backup of working files.
- If you're ready to configure a complete backup solution, take a moment to also permanently archive old files and delete them from your computer.
- When choosing an online backup plan, you can opt to save

- only selected files and folders, or types of files
  (such as music or photos)
- all files and folders
- a complete image of your disk

V. RECOMMENDED TOOLS AND SERVICES

- Acronis Backup & Recovery (file and folder backup)
- Acronis TrueImage (drive imaging backup)
- Amazon Cloud Drive (file-syncing)
- Backblaze (backup)
- Box (file-syncing)
- Carbonite (backup)
- CrashPlan (backup)
- CX.com (file-syncing)
- Dropbox (file-syncing)
- Genie Backup Manager (file and folder backup)
- Google Drive (file-syncing)
- IDrive (backup)
- IDriveSync (file-syncing)
- Jungle Disk (backup)
- MiMedia (backup)
- Mozy (backup)
- Nomadesk (backup)
- Norton Ghost (drive imaging backup)
- Norton Online Backup (backup)
- Paragon Hard Disk Manager Suite (drive imaging backup)
- Paragon Backup & Recovery (file and folder backup)
- Rebit.(file and folder backup)

- SafeSync for Home (file-syncing)
- ShadowProtect Desktop (drive imaging backup)
- SOS Online Backup (backup)
- SpiderOak (backup)
- SugarSync (file-syncing)

- Additional Content -

Archiving vs. Backing Up vs. Syncing: What's the Difference?

What's the difference between archiving files, backing them up, and syncing them?

Archiving. Archiving is what you do with files that you never intend to change again. In other words, you save the original. One example is the original copy of a photo. You might make additional copies of the image to crop, enhance the color, and edit in other ways, but you likely want to preserve the original. Receipts from e-filing your taxes are another example. You need to keep them, and you would never alter them.

Archiving might also imply that your chances of ever needing to access the files again are low, although that part is up to you.

Backing up. Technically speaking, backing up means "making a copy." Archiving is a kind of backing up, as is syncing your files. Semantically speaking, however, backing up typically refers to making a copy of data that changes somewhat frequently. For example, if you have a program that backs up your computer automatically to an external hard drive, you'll likely have the option to set how often it will back up. Once a day? Once a minute? Once a week?

BUSINESS: In a business setting, the IT department typically backs up all the company's data at least once every 24 hours, which means the company probably doesn't have the most recently updated copy of all your files at every moment. But it probably does have the most recent version as of 12:01AM that day (or whenever the backup system runs; it's often during the night).

Syncing. File-syncing is another method of backing up, although that's not its primary stated purpose. File-syncing services, such as Dropbox and Box, store copies of files in the cloud (that is to say, on a remote server that you access through the Internet) as you're working on them, provided you're connected to the Internet. These services were developed so that users could get at their files and edit them regardless of what computer they were using at the moment.

Let's say I wrote a draft of a company memo on my office computer, but when I get home I remember an important change that I need to make to the text. I want to make it now so I don't forget. If I have a file-syncing service in place, I can access that same document right from my home computer. As I edit the file, the syncing service will update the version it has in the cloud, and it will send those changes to the file residing on my office computer, too, the next time I boot up my office PC and connect it to the Internet.

7

What is the Cloud, and Do You Need It?

This chapter is a bit of a departure from others in this book. Instead of guiding you through how to set up a well-organized system or provide you with tips for better managing data, it's more of an explanation about "the cloud"—what it is and why it's useful. If you are already totally familiar with this buzzy term, feel free to skim this chapter or just look through the take-aways at the end to make sure you're not missing anything.

The cloud is one of those things that's a whole lot more confusing than it should be or needs to be. In all likelihood, you already use the cloud every day, from accessing Gmail to chatting on Facebook Messenger. All "the cloud" really means is that you are using some service that is hosted by another company in another place, which you access through the Internet. It's really not that complicated, and it's really not that new.

The cloud offers convenience above all else, but only if you have good and reliable access to the Internet. Using the cloud works best when you know when and how often your computer, smartphone, tablet, and all your other devices will be able to connect to the Internet and have good service. For many people in developed countries in particular, Internet service isn't a problem. Even if you're out and about with your mobile device all day long, you might plan to have a regular Wi-Fi connection the moment you get home or arrive at the office. If, however, you live in a place where you don't have reliable Internet access at regularly scheduled intervals, using cloud services will probably be much more difficult. It's still possible, but it could be very frustrating.

I personally use the cloud in both my work and personal life across a number of services and devices. It holds me and my work together no matter where I am or what machine I'm using.

Fears about using the cloud generally boil down to security concerns. It is hard to know precisely who has access to your information, or how much visibility they have. If a cloud company is hosting millions of users' data, isn't that database more valuable for a hacker to try and crack than the small amount of information stored on your own personal computer? Is the information in the cloud encrypted, and if so, at what point is it unencrypted so that you can see it? It's hard to know what's what.

You don't need to know every technical detail of how each cloud service works in order to feel safe using them, use them effectively, and reap their benefits. I'll try to walk you through the basics, step-by-step.

I. USING THE CLOUD FOR BACKUP AND SYNCING: WHAT IT ALL MEANS

In Chapter 6, I reviewed some different services that let you back up your computer and data to the cloud. I also briefly explained the difference between file-syncing services and cloud-based backup services.

Think of cloud-based services as those that make a copy of your computer and its data, and stick it in a lockbox or safe away from your home. Everything inside that box remains intact in case of an emergency. If your hard drive were to fail, you could go to the lockbox and pull out the spare. Of course, what's inside the safe is only as updated as the last time you made a copy and put it there; as a result, most cloud backup services let you schedule how often you make a new copy. The services typically let you save a new and updated copy as often as you like—once a day, once an hour, etc.

Cloud-based syncing services, on the other hand, work a little differently. Did you ever email yourself a file from work so that you would have it at home, or vice versa? Cloud-based syncing services basically make sure you never have to do that again. You install a program locally on your computers, smartphones, and tablets that tells the service which files and folders you want to be made available to you wherever you are.

For example, I might have a folder called "2013 Projects" on my work computer, and I want to make sure that when I'm traveling I can get to all the files in that folder no matter where I am, no matter what device I'm using, and no matter if my work computer is turned on or off. What I could do is install the same cloud-based file-syncing program on my laptop, and then tell program to always put on my laptop all the files from the "2013 Projects" folder. Now, if I work on the files from the office—and my computer is connected to the Internet at least before I shut it down when I'm done—then all the updated files will appear on my laptop as soon as I boot it up and connect it to the Internet. I don't have to go into a Web browser to get the files. They will be on my laptop, and they will be updated.

Figure 7-1: File-syncing services, such as SugarSync, shown here, let you access the most recent version of all your files from any Internet-connected computer or mobile device.

If I work on those files on my laptop—and I make sure my laptop connects to the Internet at least right before I shut it down—then all the files will magically update on my office computer the next time I boot it up and connect it to the Internet.

Now, let's say I'm in a bind. I'm visiting a friend and I left all my devices at home, but I suddenly remember a very important change I need to make to a file, and I'd rather just make that change now than write a note to remind myself to do it later. I could use my friend's computer, go online to the file-syncing service website, and log in to my account from a Web portal, where

I will see all my files in the last state that I saved them. With some services I might be able to edit the file right in the browser, but other services might require me to download the file locally to my friend's computer, open it, make the change, and then re-upload it back to the file-syncing Web portal. In either case, the next time I open my laptop or start up my office computer and connect those machines to the Internet, the changes that I may at my friend's house will be on the file on both machines.

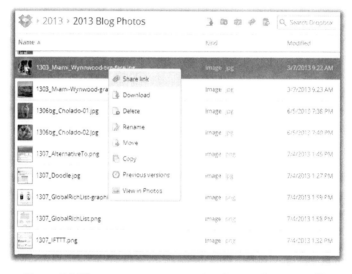

Figure 7-2: If you are on a computer that does not have your file-syncing program installed, you can still reach your files via a website, as in the case with Dropbox (shown here). You can then download your file, share it with someone else via a link, and do a few other actions with hit.

There's a little more to explain about file-syncing programs, though.

One huge mistake some people have made with file syncing

programs is deleting the source files from their computers because they believe there is a copy "in the cloud." Here's the deal. There is a copy in the cloud, but the service is looking to your computers for instruction on what to do with the file. If you update the file, the cloud service will accordingly update the file it keeps in the cloud, too. If you delete the file, the service will take that as instructions to also delete its copy of the same file. Make sense? In other words, what happens in "the cloud" mirrors what happens on your computer, tablet, or smartphone, or wherever you have installed the file-syncing program.

Stay with me, here. It's about to get slightly more complicated. It will make sense at the end, though, I promise.

Okay. I said in Chapter 6 that file-syncing services can act as a kind of backup. But how does that work if the moment you delete the files from your machine, they also delete from the cloud? I'm going to tell you using an example that actually happened to me.

I had set up SugarSync on my office laptop and home computer to make work files available to me at home. In 2012, my office laptop died. On the day it died, I had been working as normal, connected by a cable to the Internet. Before the machine failed, SugarSync had been watching all the changes I made to all my files, and it sent those changes to the cloud. SugarSync saw my hard drive failure as nothing more than my computer being shut down for the day. It didn't know that something had gone wrong. So it still had copies of all my files as they were in their most recently updated states.

I was able to go to another computer, log in to the SugarSync website, and download everything that had saved in my account. Now, those downloaded files were not synced. They were just a packet that I grabbed from the Web portal, frozen in time as they were right before my computer died. And in that scenario, it was exactly the kind of backup I needed. Sure, I had to set up Sugar-Sync all over again when I got a new office computer, but at least all those files were saved in an up-to-date state. That's the invaluable power of backing up.

One final note: When the folks from the IT department at my office retrieved the old laptop and took it into their lair to try to revive it, I told them, "Listen. I had a file-syncing program on there. If, in trying to resurrect this machine, you connect it to the Internet, the program is going to look at the computer for instructions on what to do with my files. I've already taken care of that, though, and I don't want that program to make any more changes. I want it to believe that this computer was turned off and is never being turned on again. So, if you do revive the machine, please do not connect it to the Internet until you've wiped it completely." Needless to say, it all worked out just fine.

II. THE CLOUD AND MOBILE DEVICES

So far, all my examples of how to use the cloud have revolved around laptops and desktop computers, but the cloud is just as useful and magnificent (I really do think it's "magnificent") on smartphones and tablets. Think about all those photos you take on your smartphone. Where do you put them? How diligent are you about moving them off of your phone and into a secure location where it's easier to share them and organize them, maybe so you can incorporate them into a project later, like a custom-made wall calendar? If you set up some kind of cloud-based solution for backup or syncing, all your photos from graduations and birthdays and bachelor parties (surely you want to be extra careful about where those photos end up) will automatically go to a secure place.

All the big-name smartphone operating system makers (Google, Apple, Microsoft, and RIM) include some kind of cloud solution that works in tandem with your phone. Apple has iCloud, which, for example, can automatically sync all listings in your address book on your phone to the Contacts app on your Mac, and vice versa. If you use your phone to connect to Facebook to grab all your friends' phone numbers and email addresses, all that information also goes to your Mac. Let's take Android for another example. On an Android phone, you can turn on a setting that ensures all the photos you take automatically save to your Google+ account.

And of course, all the benefits of syncing files between your office and home computers is applicable on tablets and phones as well. If you use a service like Dropbox, Box.com, SugarSync, or any of the others, you will probably want to install their apps on your little devices as well. That way, if you're standing on a subway platform for a train that never seems to come and are late to a meeting, you can use your phone to send your presentation for the meeting directly to a colleague, even when the file resides on a laptop that's at the office.

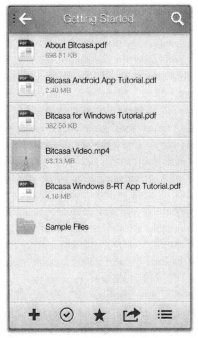

Figure 7-3: Installing a file-syncing service on a mobile device, such as the Bitcasa app for iPhone shown here, gives you access to your files

even when you don't have a computer at hand. You can usually see files and share them, but you can't always edit them.

A lot of this stuff is baked into phones and tablets already, but sometimes you need to flip some switches before it's enabled.

In Chapter 10 you'll find a lot of advice on how to manage and organize your phone. I'll discuss the things you should be saving elsewhere through the cloud so that you can remove that data from your phone and thus not bog it down with unnecessary files and information.

III. PRIVACY AND SECURITY

Hopefully I've so far convinced you that "the cloud," though slightly confusing at times, gives you unparalleled convenience. I use the cloud all over the place, and it's hard now to imagine living without it. Once you get accustomed to how it works and learn to rely on services, you can see through hindsight just how disorganized your former methods of keeping files backed up or synced were.

But the cloud isn't all puffed-up glory. There can be a dark interior to that silver cloud lining.

Anyone who holds "the cloud" in disdain and actively chooses not to use it is almost definitely concerned with one thing: privacy. Putting information online, even when that online system is private, locked, and encrypted, is never 100 percent foolproof safe. Data breaches happen. They've happened to some of my favorite services. They will continue to happen. Usernames and passwords could be leaked or hacked (please, please, please read Chapter 5 about passwords and learn how to at least minimize the pain of getting hacked). Some poor integration between two or more services could leave holes open. Stuff goes wrong. I am willing to pay the cost of the potential risks for the convenience that the cloud enables, but not everyone is.

There are many more secure and private ways to achieve the same end, but they usually require slightly more tech savvy and come with fewer conveniences or at a higher monetary cost. You could set up your own private VPN to effectively make files available to you from anywhere, but it takes work and time and research. My guess is that most people who are reading a book about organization aren't willing to invest a lot into making sure everything they have is 100 percent safe (or maybe they think they do, but have been procrastinating putting something into place for the last two years).

My advice is to keep it simple, keep your passwords unique and strong, and trade in that very small risk that something could go wrong for the convenience of a major cloud-based solution for keeping your data backed up and easily accessible. Also, if you don't put anything that's ultra-sensitive into the cloud, then the risk of having your cloud data compromised is even less pressing.

IV. TAKE-AWAYS

- "The cloud" is nothing more than a buzzword for services that use the Internet in some capacity and generally include some kind of storage.
- The primary benefits of using cloud services are convenience and accessibility, meaning you can get at your files, photos, music, and other data at any time from virtually any Internet-enabled device.
- Cloud-based file-syncing programs are not the same as cloud-based backup solutions. If you use a file-syncing program and delete files from your computer or other device, they will also be deleted from the cloud.

- Cloud-based solutions are inherently risky, at least a little bit. For most people who are trying to become more organized, the benefits of using them far outweigh the risks.
- You can protect yourself from the inherent risks of cloud services by not putting your most sensitive data in the cloud.

V. RECOMMENDED CLOUD AND FILE-SYNCING SERVICES

- Amazon Cloud Drive
- Apple iCloud, Photo Stream, iTunes Match
- Bitcasa
- Box.com
- CX
- Dropbox
- Google Drive
- IDriveSync
- Microsoft SkyDrive
- SafeSync for Home or SafeSync for Business
- SugarSync

- Additional Content -

5 Things You Probably Should Not Put in the Cloud

Any time you put data into the cloud, whether you're using Google Drive (formerly Google Docs) to save copies of documents you're actively writing or Dropbox to make all the files on your computer accessible to you from anywhere, you ought to be cognizant of whether any of those files require more special care. Certain documents need to be kept under lock and key. Here are five things you're probably better off not saving to the cloud:

1. Social Security numbers or other government-issued identity codes
2. scanned copies of passports
3. scanned birth certificates
4. files that contain unencrypted bank account numbers
5. an unencrypted list of your usernames and passwords

For items 4 and 5, it's worth knowing that online bank accounts, personal finance software and apps, and password managers encrypt information such as the full bank account number and your passwords. Any bank or password manager product should be verified by a third-party security agency, such as VeriSign, that certifies these sensitive materials are kept encrypted. But if you scan personal documents, such as an old tax report that you filed by paper mail, those kinds of numbers will just appear on a PDF or whatever format you use totally unencrypted. To be really safe, it's better to keep those kinds of files backed up by a more secure method, which might include burning them to disc or an external hard drive.

III

Part III: Mobile

8

Setting Up Your Smartphone to Become an Organizational Tool

Every now and again, I chuckle at the term "smartphone." My smartphone's "phone" capabilities probably account for less than 10 percent of my total usage of it. This little device of mine is a pocket PC, pure and simple, and you'd be hard-pressed to pry it out of my hands on an average day. Mind you, I'm not an obsessed cell phone nut who can't even get through dinner without looking at the screen. While on vacation, I go whole days with my phone switched off entirely. But during the day-in day-out grind, I see the possibilities for my phone to keep me organized and help me be the person I want to be, and by golly if I don't make use of it.

A smartphone goes everywhere with you. It can remind you of things you need to do based on the date and time, or your location. The old excuse for not writing down important information, "I don't have a pen," no longer applies. When you get to the post office to mail a package to your sister days before her birthday, rest assured her address is at your fingertips. Trying to lose weight? Pick up a calorie-counting app or exercise-logging app, and you'll be able to check in on your own progress throughout the day at a moment's notice. At the grocery store and can't remember what you need to buy? Luckily, you can keep an ongoing list on your smartphone that never gets stuck to the bottom of the shopping cart and isn't full of cross-outs and eraser marks. Did you forget to make a dinner reservation for your anniversary? You can read up on restaurants and reserve a table from your phone in about a minute. Missing a big sports game because you're at your nephew's bar mitzvah? You can quietly and discreetly check in on the score with any number of apps, mobile websites, and services. Not that I'm saying you should. But you could.

This chapter, as well as Chapters 9 and 10, get down to the nitty-gritty about how to use your smartphone as an organizational tool, what you might want to keep on your smartphone, and what kinds of things you should regularly delete from it.

To get started, let's talk about basic settings you might want to enable, as they are foundational for reaping some of the other benefits of having a smartphone in the first place.

I. WHAT TO ENABLE ON YOUR SMARTPHONE

iPhones, Android phones, and pretty much all other major smartphones have a few settings or features that you'll want to enable.

Passcode or Other Security Lock

Every phone should give you the option to add a passcode or some kind of security barrier. If for some odd reason your smartphone does not have this feature, get a new phone. You should absolutely have a passcode enabled on your phone.

Some phones support nothing more than simple four-digit PINs. Others give you the choice of using different security measures, such as a passphrase or even a gesture code, such as using your finger on screen to draw two circles with a line bisecting them, or whatever you motion you set. And the iPhone 5s has an optional fingerprint scanner built into the home button.

Every single smartphone owner should lock his or her phone. Period. A lot of sensitive information could be residing on your phone, from your home address to pictures of your children, and you do not want to leave all that information open to a perpetrator. Set a passcode, and don't share it with anyone other than maybe your partner.

I'm of the mind that even children should not have a parent's phone's passcode. Perhaps you think your kids should have it in the event of an emergency. Well, they can use the "emergency call" feature, which does not require unlocking the phone. You could instead make them memorize the phone numbers of emergency services and immediate family members. But I'm not in the business of giving child-rearing advice. My point is you should keep your phone passcode very well guarded.

Find My Phone

All the major smartphones have some kind of service that helps you find a lost phone or erase everything on it from a Web account if you think it's been stolen. On some phones, the feature is built in and you just have to enable it. On others, you have to download an app.

On the iPhone, it's called Find My iPhone, and you can turn it on by going to

Settings > iCloud > Find My iPhone

Figure 8-1: The Find My iPhone feature helps you locate a lost iPhone, or remotely erase it for added security if you believe it to be stolen.

I'll go into more detail about iCloud a little later.

Android users have their pick of third-party apps for this feature, including Wheres My Droid [sic], Find My Phone, and Locate My Droid.

Here's how these services work.

Let's say you misplaced your phone, but you're pretty sure it's somewhere in your friend's car. You can log onto any computer and send your iPhone a command to play a loud sound, or flash on screen a message, like, "Hey Ana! If you see this, please call me! 212-555-1234. Thanks! Jill."

Or, perhaps you can't find your phone, but you're pretty sure you left it either at the office or at a restaurant. You can log in to that Web account and see where your phone is on a map.

If you fear the worst and think your iPhone was stolen, you can choose an option to erase all the information on your phone.

These services generally only work when you have GPS, also known as "location services," enabled as well. GPS can drain the battery, so there are times when you'll probably want to turn it off for the battery's sake. Also, the "find my phone" feature doesn't work if your phone's battery runs dry. These are the tough problems facing smartphone owners (that was intended with an air of sarcasm).

Regardless, figure out which "find my phone" options you have for your particular phone, and enable them. Give yourself a minute or two to test it so you're familiar with how it works, too. You wouldn't want to be in a position of needing this service and not knowing how to use it.

GPS

Get familiar with the GPS setting on your phone: where it is and how to toggle it on and off. GPS is the switch I turn on and off the most on my phone. It's a brilliant and invaluable feature for so many uses, but when I'm out for a long day and need to conserve battery power, GPS is the first thing I shut off.

Backup

Another built-in feature on most phones is the ability to back up its data automatically and usually over Wi-Fi (that would be a "cloud service," as explained in Chapter 7). Some people prefer to back up their phones to a computer, as it generally can hold more data than what's allotted in a free cloud service.

When you first bought your phone, you probably set up some kind of backup solution, although you may have since forgotten what it is, how often it backs up, and to where.

Take a moment to review your backup settings and options. Better yet, take a moment to figure out how to back up your phone right now.

On an iPhone, go to

Settings > iCloud > Storage & Backup

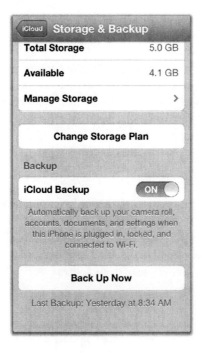

Figure 8-2: From the iCloud Storage & Backup page in an iPhone's Settings, you can see whether iCloud is enabled. iCloud is Apple's included backup plan for iPhones and iPads. This page also shows how much storage space remains in your account.

At the bottom, you can see the time and date of your most recent backup.

On an Android phone, it's a little more complicated because there is no native backup option for your entire phone. But you can back up the most essential data using Google. Go to

Settings > Privacy

and check the boxes for "Back up my settings" or it might be called "Back up and reset" or something similar, and find "Automatic restore," as Android devices tend to have slight variations in language between different models.

Figure 8-3: Android's backup settings let you back up some data from your phone, although you can use a backup app on Android as well.

Then go to

Settings > Accounts and sync

Here, you can choose your Google account and select the options you want. I recommend backing up system settings, contacts, and apps at the very least.

Syncing

If you read Chapter 7, you know that backup and syncing are not the same thing, but that they are in fact related. On a smartphone, the blurry line between backup and syncing gets even fuzzier.

Built-in syncing services that come with your phone, such as the ability to automatically sync photos from an Android phone to Google+ or an iPhone to Photo Stream, are different from other file-syncing services. When you "sync" data from your smartphone, very often you are creating an actual backup of that data. In the previous chapter, I warned you that if you use a file-syncing service and then you delete the files from your computer, they will also be deleted from the file-syncing service. With smartphones, that's not always the case.

The next two chapters will go into more detail about how to use syncing services, and when you should keep data such as photos on your phone versus when you can delete it to free up space.

In terms of third-party syncing apps like the ones mentioned at the end of Chapter 7—if you use a service for your office and home computers and have in it files that you could ostensibly need while you're out and about or traveling, install the app for that service on your phone. But, be quite selective about the amount of data you chose to have synced locally to the phone. If you're too liberal, the syncing app will eat up all your phone's available space, and you won't have anything left for all the important to-do lists, family calendar, personal finance information, and other great stuff that I explore in the next chapter.

With a syncing app installed on your phone, you can always get to the files you need via the Internet, even with a cellular (3G, 4G, LTE, etc.) data connection. It may take a little longer to retrieve remotely stored and synced files than if you had them saved and synced locally on your phone, but oftentimes the purpose of having a file-syncing app on your phone is for emergencies.

Now don't confuse that use case (the one in which you need a file from your office computer in a pinch) with using third-party syncing apps to upload files kept natively on your phone to the cloud-based syncing services. Just as you can turn on iCloud or settings on an Android phone to back up your photos and contacts, you can set a third-party syncing services to sync files from your phone.

All these options for syncing and backup can start to get pretty messy very quickly. It's easy to forget what you put where. It's the source of so many people's disorganization on a smartphone. The next section will give you a simple yet powerful strategy for managing all those services you use so that you never confuse them.

II. COMPARTMENTALIZATION

As a notoriously compartmentalized person, I use compartmentalization strategies to organize practically everything. On my smartphone, it's how I remember where everything is, as well as a way for me to stay sane in terms of keeping my work and personal lives separate.

For example, on my personal iPhone, I use Apple's Mail app for only personal email. I keep my business email, on the other hand, strictly refined to a third-party app, in this case, the Gmail app because my business uses Google for email services. Likewise, in selecting a task-management and to-do app, it was crucial for me to find one that included support for "folders" so that I could have a personal to-do list that's kept completely separate from my work to-do list.

Compartmentalizing is nothing more than creating a series of simple rules, such as "only personal photos should be saved locally on the phone; all work-related photos must be uploaded to service X and deleted from the phone immediately."

Thus, as a rule, I keep personal photos on my phone and sync them to my home computer using Photo Stream. When I need to take photos for work (for me that usually involves taking screenshots of different apps while I test them), I only do it while at work and I immediately upload them to my office computer, and then I file them right away into the folders where they belong. Then I immediately delete them from my phone. Work images do not belong on the phone. Period. That's the rule I gave myself. (This rule comes with an extra benefit: It makes it very difficult for me to work during my time off when I'm home. Once rules become ingrained in my own psyche, I find it very hard to rail against them.)

I compartmentalize my file-syncing services, too. I use Dropbox for personal files, SugarSync for work files, and Google Drive for home documents that I need to share with my partner, such as financial spreadsheets. Having dedicated spaces for different kinds of content makes it easier to find them, too, especially on a mobile device.

III. HOW CAN YOUR SMARTPHONE HELP YOU BE MORE ORGANIZED?

So far, this chapter has dealt with setting up your smartphone so that it is organized, which indeed is the first step. You won't get very far without first having that foundation in place.

But the more important question is: How can your smartphone help you be more organized?

I'm guessing that you already use your smartphone a good deal. It could very well be the first thing you hear every morning if it doubles as your alarm clock, and certainly it can help guide you through your day with its included GPS mapping capabilities, calendar reminders, and much more.

There is a fine line between leveraging a smartphone to make use of all its abilities, and relying on it too much. Your pocket PC can and should guide you, steer you back on track when you veer off course, and prompt you toward executing more ideal behaviors and habits, but the real change to be more organized has to start inside you. You need to work toward a lifestyle of greater organization in order for your phone be by your side as an assistant on that journey.

In the next chapter, I'll list the apps that I think are essential companions on this journey toward becoming more organized. But know that you have to be in control of the apps. The apps aren't there to make you be more organized. They're more like signposts along the way.

IV. TAKE-AWAYS

- Because a smartphone goes with you everywhere, it is an ideal tool for helping you stay organized throughout the day, every day.
- In order for a smartphone to be an effective tool in your organization toolkit, you must first enable a few settings and features that will help it do its part of the job.
- When it comes to managing all the various data you keep on your smartphone, remember that one simple way to organize it is to compartmentalize it. Use different apps, services, folders, and so on to separate different kinds of files or data.
- Don't become dependent on a smartphone for organization. Think of it more like a guiding light to get you where you want to be with your organizational habits.

9

What to Keep on a Smartphone

The combination to my gym locker is saved in a note on my phone. I also have the Wi-Fi network name and password for my sister's house and a family friend's house, two places where, more than once, I found myself unable to get onto the Internet while I was visiting and everyone else was asleep. My bicycle's serial number is saved as a photo in my phone, in case the bike is stolen and the police ask me for it. I also have the serial numbers of my computers and iPhone.

Knowing that I have all these little bits of information in one place brings me enormous peace of mind. I've essentially offloaded them from my brain to a place where I trust they will always be. In the same way some people have a routine for putting their keys in a dish or on a hook, the same exact place every time they step through the door, I put important information onto my phone. I never question whether my keys are where I always put them or whether the itinerary for my next upcoming flight is on my phone. They are. I know they are. I trust that I have some autopilot setting in me that puts my keys and that itinerary in their respective places every single time, whether I actively remember doing so or not. It's routine. It's habit. I trust myself to put things where they belong.

The more you use a smartphone—and I mean really use it—the more you'll build habits for 1) putting all these important pieces of information onto your phone and 2) referring to them when you need them. Habits can be manual, but some of those same tasks can be automated, too. For example, there are apps that find travel confirmation messages in your email and automatically save all the relevant info into the app itself, adding flight-tracking updates in the process.

This chapter explores the kinds of things you might want to keep on your smartphone to be more organized. It has a lot of advice on how to do it and which apps to use. Each section goes into quite a bit of detail, and they don't cover everything under the sun, but rather hit on some universal concepts that apply to most people. Here's an overview:

- lists and notes
- calendar, contacts, email
- important files and a file-syncing app
- money-management and baking apps
- health and fitness apps
- entertainment: photos, music, podcasts, games, sports apps

iPhone users might also be interested in reading more detailed tips about how to arrange apps in an organized way on their home screens, contained in the Additional Content at the end of this chapter.

I. LISTS AND NOTES

I have a saying: "A looked-at list is a used list."

Any list you make becomes more valuable the more you refer to it. The same holds true for notes. The act of writing certainly helps reinforce information on its own, but the whole point of a list or note is reference. So how do you get yourself to remember to look at your own lists and notes more?

My lists and notes became much more valuable and manageable since I bought my first smartphone. I believe a huge reason it happened is because I look at my phone dozens of times a day. The more you look at your phone, the more likely you are to see those list apps and note apps staring you back in the face. If you see them, you'll open them.

The most obvious kinds of lists to keep are to-do lists and shopping lists. Neither has to be boring or typical.

To-do Lists

To-do lists can be supremely powerful little assistants, but only if you build them well and use them effectively. So often I see poorly written to-do lists, and it makes me batty—what a wasted opportunity! (See the Additional Content at the end of this chapter for tips on how to write a better to-do list.) A to-do list may sound trivial, but it's central to completing tiny steps that help you achieve much larger and more important goals. They go way beyond taking out the trash and signing your kid's permission slips.

If you're a highly disorganized person, you probably feel pretty bad about your to-do lists. They don't get you anywhere, and there could be a few reasons. For starters, you could be setting yourself up for failure because of the nature of your to-do list. Or it could be that you are not dedicated to the list itself for any number of reasons, some perhaps quite trivial. When I used to keep paper to-do lists, I had days when I didn't want to look at them because the paper was ugly, filled with cross outs and written in atrocious handwriting (that would be mine). I remember copying my to-do lists onto new scraps of paper sometimes two or three times a day just try to make them look neater and more palatable. Let me make this perfectly clear: I hated my to-do lists for very superficial reasons.

Putting my tasks into a list on my phone immediately solved half the things I didn't like about my lists. I could now type them and use an attractive typeface. Cross-outs became a thing of the past. I could edit an existing list rather than rewrite the whole dang thing. And all these very minor things amounted to me liking my lists more.

Figure 9-1: A task-management app, such as Any.do, is essential for making use of your smartphone as an organizational tool.

I've used the same app, Awesome Note, for my to-do lists for about three years. As of this writing, it's available on iPhone, iPad, and Galaxy Note. It meets a few of my important requirements:

- I like the way it looks.
- I can keep multiple lists separate from one another (it uses folders, which are color-coded).
- It includes deadlines and reminder settings.
- It has a calendar view.
- It syncs with other services that I also use.

I've also spent a lot of time recently using a newer to-do app called Any.do, which has a very different look and feel. Any.do includes one really neat feature called the Any.do Moment, which reminds you at the same time every day to review your upcoming to-dos. I love that this feature encourages you to create a habit out of looking over your tasks and revising their due dates regularly. For anyone who has struggled to keep up with a to-do list in the past, I highly recommend Any.do.

How does a really good to-do list look?

- *Short.* You should be able to glance at your to-do list and know in a second or two what you have to do next, as well as where your priorities lie.
- *Shaped by a clear goal.* The tasks that go on your to-do list should be in pursuit of a higher goal. If your goal has been unstated until now, take a moment to consider what it is. Implicit in this quality is the fact that it's okay—if not downright preferable—to have more than one list. You might have different lists for different projects, or some for work and some for home.
- *Contains tasks, not goals.* The items on a good to-do list should be concrete and have a "completed" state. That is to say, they're tasks and not goals. There is a state of completion for the task "Call my wife" but not for "Appreciate my wife more."
- *Marked by deadlines.* Every task should have an order of priority and a deadline. For most people, high-priority tasks have a deadline of "today." Do you need to write that down? Maybe. Maybe not.
- *Realistic.* Both the tasks you write and the deadlines you assign must be realistic and reasonable. Don't set 17 tasks as urgently due today when really only four must get done by the end of the day "or else!" If you put unrealistic deadlines on yourself, you'll hate your to-do

list because it will be a constant remind of what you haven't done.

- *Always active.* Some people joke that the first item on their to-do list is "create a to-do list." It's tongue-in-cheek, but it's actually a very good tactic. You should include items on your to-do list that you absolutely will do no matter what. Crossing off items is encouraging and motivating. You want to keep that list moving at all times.

Tip:

Create a "Someday" list or deadline setting for all the stuff that isn't really important or isn't in pursuit of a clear goal. Crossing off your tasks feels good—much better than seeing them remain on your list for weeks at a time— but more importantly, it forces you to look at your list anew and repeatedly. Every time you cross off a task, you look at your list again. And a looked-at list is a used list.

Shopping Lists

Other kinds of lists you probably want to keep on your phone are shopping lists, and these might include:

- groceries
- holiday shopping

- personal shopping (for example, clothing items you need)
- special purpose shopping (back to school, pre-vacation).

Figure 9-2: One piece of organizing information that's good to keep on a smartphone is a shopping list. This one, shown in the Awesome Note app, lets you check off items as you buy them. You can also uncheck the items when they run out at home to put frequently purchased items back on your shopping list quickly and easily.

Tip:

Keep grocery lists in an app that
uses checkboxes that you can check and

un-check. Mark them with a check when
you buy an item, and uncheck the same
box when the item runs out so it return
to your list. You'll never have to retype
frequently purchased items.

Notes

So far I've talked about to-do lists while skirting around notes. Where you put your notes, how you organize them, and how you reference them and later leverage them depends on what kind of notes you take. A lot of my notes actually fall into my to-do list, so I append them to tasks (Awesome Note has a notes option on any to-do item).

Other kinds of notes that are more free-form I keep in the note-taking and syncing service Evernote, which has apps for just about every platform you can imagine. One problem with keeping general notes in a general-purpose note-taking app is it's easy to forget they exist.

Tip:
Put your to-do app and note-keeping app
on your smartphone home screen. The more
you see it, the more you'll open it and use it.

I should mention that I use Evernote for more than just jotting down short notes. If I'm away from my desk and I have a pretty solid idea about an article I'd like to write, I might outline it in Evernote. I also keep meeting notes in Evernote because even if I have an impromptu meeting, I know I will have my phone and the Evernote app with me to take notes.

II. Calendar, Contacts, and Email

Another set of information you probably want to keep on your smartphone for the purpose of staying organized includes your calendar, contacts, and email. I lump them together because they are often interconnected, even if you use different apps to access the various pieces.

Calendar

In setting up a calendar on your phone, it's very important to know your overall calendaring or scheduling strategy. I personally don't like to save my work appointments on my iPhone's calendar. I strictly reserve that calendar for personal use. I'm a fairly strong proponent of work-life balance, so my theory is if I need to be reminded of work appointments, I want to have the work apps turned on, or be in front of my work computer to see them. In other words, I want to be able to shut them off when I don't need them (like on weekends).

I've met plenty of people who tell me they've long ago abandoned the idea of keeping their work and personal calendars separate, but before you give up all hope, ask yourself what you would like to happen. Do you really want separate calendars? It can be done. And it's not that hard, but it takes a little diligence, at least at first. But maybe you would rather have them together so that you don't overbook, which may be a consideration if you tend to work off hours.

Figure 9-3: To use your smartphone as an organizational tool, you need to have a calendar set up. It doesn't matter which calendar app or service you choose, so long as you're diligent about using it to keep track of meetings, events, or other obligations.

The stock calendar apps for Android phones and iPhones include features that let you color-code different kinds of appointments. For example you might have all your personal appointments in green and work appointments in blue. You can set the calendar so that only blue appointments are visible, and do other customizations like that.

If you like Google Calendar, you can sync to the Calendar app on iPhone, which is what I do for my personal calendar. All my work-related appointments are available to me in Outlook and via my business-related Google account, which I keep separate from my personal Google account and don't load onto my phone.

Note that your to-do lists should not go into your regular calendar. The calendar should be reserved for events, like appointments and meetings. Very important deadlines might get penciled into your calendar, but my feeling is they should for the most part remain in the task-management or to-do app.

Contacts

I definitely think the contacts feature—that is, the address book—on most phones is worth populating, and it's something you should back up as well (see Chapter 6). Both Android and iOS let you import contacts from other places so that you can very quickly compile all the email addresses and phone numbers you have from Gmail, Facebook, LinkedIn, and others sources.

If your contacts app seems to be a disastrous disarray of disorganization, check your settings before you delete entries or search for duplicates. Most smartphones give you the ability to unlink your contacts app from other sources where it's pulling information. So, for example, if you realize hundreds of Facebook friends' contact information is cluttering up your phone, it's better to unlink and unsync Facebook than try to remove people one by one.

BUSINESS TIP:

Specialty contact apps can do so
much more than the stock contact apps, especially
for business-minded people. For example, Brewster

can list for you people with whom you're losing
touch, so that you can strengthen key relationships
before it's too late. Cloze consolidates tweets,
Facebook status updates, and emails by person by
day—good for keeping an eye on what important
people in your network are doing and saying across
the social media landscape.

Email

I probably don't need to persuade most people to load their email accounts on their smartphones, but let me just quickly refresh the value of having them at your fingertips.

For me, having email on my phone is not at all about managing mail. Maybe an important incoming message will reach me quicker, or I'll be able to reply to messages that keep getting pushed to the wayside during those free moments when I'm waiting in a line, but really, email is a place I consult when I need important information and can't find it elsewhere.

If I don't find a friend's address listed in my contact management app, surely she would have sent it to me at some point via email. Or maybe I want to double-check the time of an event because I'm worried about a time zone syncing issues in my calendar—email to the rescue.

To anyone who is already overloaded with email and struggling to get a grip on it, I say: Turn off badges and notifications on your phone. If you're working on your email issues from a desktop computer or laptop, there's no need to further stress yourself out by seeing the count of unread message pile up when you're going about your day.

On the other hand, if you've waged an all-out war with email and want to open the battleground on your phone, there are some tricks you can use to stay on top of email, or dig out of it, that are exclusive to mobile devices. The Mailbox app, for example, was designed to encourage iPhone users to process email quickly and consistently. "Do something with each message," it seems to say, whether it means snoozing it temporarily from your inbox or filing it into a folder. (As of this writing, it's available for iPhone and iPad, with an Android app purportedly in development. Android users can also use Boomerang, which is similar.)

III. IMPORTANT FILES AND FILE-SYNCING APP

Of all the technology innovations that have come out since the late 1990s, file syncing is absolutely at the top of my list for things that have changed my life. I wouldn't dare have a smartphone that didn't have at least one file-syncing app on it.

Put simply, these apps give you access to important files that you might otherwise store on your home or office computer. Now flip that and reverse it: File-syncing apps also take important information that you keep or create on your phone and make them available on your computers.

Figure 9-4: Dropbox and some other file-syncing apps have a feature that lets you automatically upload photos you take with your phone to your file-syncing account, helping you back up your images and copy them to your computer as well.

If you want to be super organized with your file syncing apps, you should look into the offline storage capabilities of the app in question and your particular smartphone. Offline storage simply means that you can keep copies of some of your data locally on your phone so that you don't need an Internet connection to get them. You might, for example, have a folder called Essential Work Files that you mark to be stored offline because they contain information you might need from the road, and call it knows if you'll be able to get a signal when you're on a train somewhere between Tuscaloosa and Saskatoon.

The organizational aspect here about what files you make available via a file-syncing program all depends on what you do with the file-syncing program, rather than how you manage your smartphone. The phone is instead a vehicle for getting the information. For more on file-syncing services, see Chapter 7.

IV. MONEY-MANAGEMENT APPS

Money-management apps belong on your smartphone if you're trying to get your personal finances in order. They can remind you and alert you of your budget while you're in the act of spending money. Some can also remind you of bills that are due soon, and even let you set up payment for them no matter where you are. These include apps such as Mint and Check, which I discuss in more detail in Chapter 14.

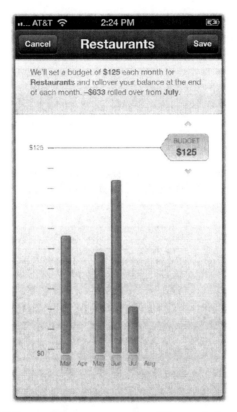

Figure 9-5: Personal finance apps such as Mint can help you stick to your budget when you're out spending money.

In addition to budgeting and bill-pay apps, you'll likely also want to add apps for the banks where you keep your spending money. They typically include a feature that lets you find nearby ATMs. They also let you look at your available balance at any time, which is more likely to be up to date than a third-party finance app such as Mint (which also shows balances in your accounts).

If you actively watch the stock market, you'll find notification options for stock alerts in iPhone, which you can customize to show the stocks you care about. The Google Search app, available on both Android phones and iPhones, also has a neat feature that lets you watch particular stocks and get customized reports if the price rises or falls to a certain level.

Other apps can save you money by showing you deals and discounts that are physically nearby, although I'm not a huge fan of these services because they promote impulse shopping, which isn't really for me. At times they are useful, though. For example, if while traveling in a city that you don't know well you need to stop for lunch, you might as well check Yelp, Foursquare, Groupon, LevelUp, or any other app that offers restaurant recommendations and discounts. It's nice to save a few bucks off your check if you were going to eat at some random café anyway.

V. HEALTH AND FITNESS APPS

I'm a huge fan of health and fitness apps. I'm lucky in that it don't have any chronic illnesses or medications that I need to take regularly. But I do like to keep an eye on my general health, and I like to have emergency first-aid and health apps at my fingertips should I ever need them.

Health

WebMD is a free app for health information and first aid. You can look up symptoms if you or someone nearby feels ill, but I think the more important value of this app is the first aid reference it provides. It's one app that I think everyone should download and hope they never have to use. I recommend exploring it a little when you first download it, though, so that if you ever do need to use it, you'll be somewhat familiar with how it works and where the information resides.

More specific ailments and conditions call for more specific apps. MyMeds, for example, helps you keep track of your medications and reminds you when you need to order refills. There are apps for tracking blood glucose levels, heart rate, blood pressure, and other vital signs. Some more comprehensive fitness apps for measuring and tracking your daily exercise (which I discuss next) include those vital sign tools within them.

Again, a huge reason having these apps on your phone helps to keep you more organized is because they're in front of your eyes on multiple occasions throughout the day, pretty much every day. The more you see these apps, the more you'll be reminded to use them, which is especially important if you have a medical condition or health issue that requires constant vigilance.

Fitness

Fitness apps generally refer to those used for exercise and healthy eating. Fitness apps are a dime a dozen, and many of them are pretty terrible or only do one thing as opposed to giving you better insight into your total overall fitness levels. A few that I like and that have worked well for me personally are:

- *MyFitnessPal.* MyFitnessPal counts calories both consumed and expended (you have to manually log exercise, from walking to more rigorous activities) to help you lose, maintain, or gain weight. You can also track your weight with this app. Of all the calorie counting apps I've seen, this one has the best database of foods.
- *Fitbit.* The Fitbit app is ideal for anyone who owns a Fitbit-brand activity tracker, but you don't actually need to own a tracker to use it. As with MyFitnessPal, you use it log foods you eat and thus count calories, while also logging your activities, sleep times, weight,

heart rate, and so forth. This app is great if you use a lot of "smart" devices, such as a Wi-Fi scale or glucose monitor, because it connects to a number of other gadgets to automate some of the process. The Fitbit app is surprisingly comprehensive.

- *Argus.* Argus basically turns your phone into an all-day activity-tracking device by using the GPS feature to measure how much you walk or run in a day. Big warning: Argus drains the phone's battery (unless you're using it on an iPhone 5s, which makes use of a unique motion coprocessor), so use it with caution. It also includes features for tracking how much water you drink and what foods you eat, although it doesn't contain any calorie counting features, so it's much more lightweight than the other apps I've mentioned so far. Argus is good app to play with if you are flirting with the idea of buying a fitness tracker but aren't sold on the concept yet.

- *Running and other sport apps.* If you run, surely you have heard of the many excellent runners' apps on the market: Runtastic, MapMyRun, Runmeter, Nike+ Running. Some of the brands behind these apps also make more general fitness tracking apps (MapMyFitness, for example), as well as sport-specific apps (Cyclemeter, for example).

- *At-home exercise apps.* Finally, there are apps that help you work out at home. Two I like are GAIN Fitness and Touchfit: GSP, which both contain basic routines that work on cardio, strength, and flexibility. Apps for yoga, Pilates, and other specialty workouts are also worthwhile if you prefer those kinds of exercise.

VI. ENTERTAINMENT: PHOTOS, MUSIC, PODCASTS, GAMES

Mobile entertainment is serious business. I roll my eyes whenever people try to convince me that using a smartphone to listen to music or podcasts, play games, or look at photos is frivolous. It's not. Those activities are part of how we enjoy our lives.

The next chapter deals with keeping your smartphone clean and organized in the sense of knowing what to delete from it and when, and the entertainment category accounts for a lot of that content. So here I'm just going to give few quick tips on how to organize the content in those different subcategories—but bear in mind that the real organizing efforts for them is more about how you delete and reinstall the content rather than order the existing stuff.

Photos

The camera on a smartphone is one of the best tools in an organizational tool belt. Photos can capture a whole lot more than just faces and landscapes. I've already mentioned that I take photos of important information, such as the serial number of my bicycle, which I then save to a note-syncing program (Evernote) to make it available to me from any Internet-connected device.

Tip:

Take a screenshot of your phone's serial number or other identifier, which you can usually find in the settings. Save it to a secure syncing program. You'll need this information if the phone is ever stolen.

———

I definitely recommend sorting photos into albums, and I definitely recommend creating an album called "Headshots" or "Profile pictures" where you save a recent photo of yourself that you can use when you sign up for new app accounts from your phone and need to add a picture. As you'll read in Chapter 13 about social media, I also recommend using one consistent profile photo across most if not all of your accounts, particularly if you are trying to project a professional image.

There are a few more tips on managing photos from a smartphone in Chapter 11 about photos, including the suggestion to turn on syncing, either in the form of the syncing that's included with your phone (Photo Stream in iCloud for iOS users, Google+ Photos for Android users, or an alternative app and service that includes an "automatic upload" feature). Syncing your photos ensures that all the images you snap from your smartphone also appear on your computer on in a cloud-based account.

———

BUSINESS TIP:
During or at the end of a business meeting, you can take snapshots of whiteboards or important slides from a presentation. I recommend saving those photos to another program that can run optical character recognition (OCR) technology on them to make the text contained in the images searchable and readable. Evernote can do that job, as well as let you add more

information about the meeting to make the
notes easier to find, such as tags that
describe the content of the meeting, the
names of the participants, and geo-location
information if you're the kind of person
who recalls information based on
where you were when you received it.

Music

Managing the music that goes onto your phone is best done on
your computer (and in the case of the iPhone, is the only way you
can really manage the music on your phone). I think the real trick
is to not keep too much music on your phone, but rather to have
an organized strategy for adding and removing it at regular intervals, which is a large part of the next chapter, and I won't spoil it
here.

Podcasts

As an avid podcast listener, I almost have a hard time classifying
them as "entertainment." I use podcasts to keep in touch with the
news and what's happening in the world. (Because I'm a writer
who stares at a screen all day long and suffer from eye fatigue and
poor vision, I rely on podcasts and other audio output for content
that other people might read.)

Most podcast apps have features for subscribing to shows so
that new episodes automatically download, which you may want
to enable for some shows, but perhaps not all. Some, such as
Stitcher Radio, give you tools for organizing shows into "stations"
or sets (I think of them as folders). Use these features, and be dili-

gent about turning on that automatic download feature, as it's the one that will get you into the most disorganization trouble.

Games

Should you keep games on your smartphone at all? Sure! Games stimulate the brain and add playfulness to our lives. They teach us and give us new avenues for socialization. If you think video games are a waste of time, you probably haven't played many in the last decade.

If you don't want to be tempted to play games too often, however, keep game apps on your last home screen, and preferably in a folder so that you don't see them regularly. If you share your phone with other family members—for example, you hand your phone to a kid who plays more games on the phone than you do—be sure to turn on any controls that limit or prevent in-app purchases.

VII. TAKE-AWAYS

- A smartphone is an invaluable tool for staying organized in part because it's almost always with you and because you look at it frequently.
- Because most people look at their phones many times throughout the day, it's an ideal place for keeping things you need to remember, which might include to-do tasks, lists, notes, reminders to take medications, calendar appointments, your budget and upcoming bills due, and much more.
- Use file-syncing and note-syncing apps to make important information available to you from your

phone, but also from any other device you might happen to have at your disposal.

- Do keep entertainment apps and content on your phone, and put those apps either in sight or out of sight, depending on how frequently you want to visit them.

VIII. APP RECOMMENDATIONS

- Any.do
- Argus
- Asana
- Awesome Note (+To-Do/Calendar)
- Bitcasa
- Boomerang (only for Android)
- Brewster
- Cloze
- EasilyDo
- Evernote
- Fitbit
- Foursquare
- GAIN Fitness
- Google Search
- Groupon
- LevelUp
- Mailbox (only for iPhone, iPad; Android app due out soon)
- MapMyRun, MapMyFitness
- MyFitnessPal
- Nike+ Running

- Runmeter, Cyclemeter
- Runtastic
- Todoist
- Touchfit: GSP
- TripIt
- WebMD
- Yelp

- Additional Content -

How to Write Better To-Do Lists

How effective is your to-do list? Do you gleefully cross things off it throughout the day, or does it fill you with dread and remind you of everything you haven't done?

A good to-do list should be fulfilling—not be a source of despair. There's one major trick to making better to-do lists that comes down to understanding the difference between goals, objectives, and tasks.

Goals are big picture achievements or desired outcomes. A goal might be "become fluent in Hindi," or "create the best website in Canada for outdoor sports e-commerce." They're usually difficult to quantify. How "fluent" is fluent? By whose measure does the site have to "the best?"

Objectives are markers along the way to reaching a goal. Objectives are quantifiable and usually much easier to define than goals. An example of an objective might be "have a five-minute conversation with a Hindi speaker," or "increase Canadian outdoor enthusiast website audience by 20 percent this year."

Tasks are the actions one takes to reach an objective. They are often single events, although they can repeat. A task might be "learn three new Hindi verbs," or "tweet about the cross-country ski promotion."

Tasks are what belong on an effective to-do list.

It's still important to know what your objectives and goals are, too. If your tasks are not getting you closer to your objectives and goals, why are you wasting your time doing them?

With personal to-do lists, your goal might be something unstated, like "better manage the family budget." You know in your head that's why your to-do list contains tasks that relate to finance, but the goal might not be explicit. Take a moment to think about your unstated goals. If you know the goal, your tasks and to-do list become more meaningful. Instead of looking like a tedious list of the chores you have to get done, it becomes a clear path toward greater fulfillment.

-

- Additional Content -

3 Tips for Organizing Apps

A smartphone is only as useful as the apps you keep on it—and how quickly you can get to them when you need them. I have a few strategies for how I arrange my apps to help keep them organized, put them in easy reach of my fingers, and thus increase my efficiency by reducing the time it takes me to find the apps I use most often.

1. Use Your Hotspots

The areas of the screen in nearest reach of your fingers are also what I like to call "hotspots." If you use your thumbs to navigate your phone and are right-handed, your hotspots are probably the lower-right corner and leftmost column. I hold my phone in a slightly unusual way: in the palm of my left hand, using the middle finger of my right hand to tap and swipe (I have stiff little thumbs). As a result, my hotspots are the bottom two rows of the home screen.

You may have already utilized your hotspots, wherever they happen to fall for you, by putting your most-used apps in those locations. But if not, be sure to take advantage of those zones.

2. Cluster

The second trick is to cluster your apps. By "clustering," I mean position them near one another on the screen, but not in a folder (using folders is a different trick). You've likely already clustered your four most frequently used apps in the dock and around your primary hot spots. Clustering works in other areas, too, though.

On the second screen of my phone, I have clustered together a few social media apps: Vine, Facebook, Flickr, and Pinterest. I "hang out" in that cluster when I'm relaxing and using my phone to leisurely check out what's new. I keep them on the second screen, rather than the first, because I don't want to tempt myself into looking at those apps too frequently. I reserve the home screen for apps that are more important to me.

3. File into Folders

Folders let you group apps together and name the set while only taking up one slot on the home screen. There are two main ways to use folders: by app theme and by use.

Theme means apps that are similar to one another, such as putting all music-streaming apps together, or all games together. Usage means how or when you use the apps. Theme folders don't have to just hold apps of the same genre, though. I have a theme folder on my iPhone that lives at the top of my home screen called "Apple apps," which holds apps that came preinstalled on the phone but that I don't use frequently. An example of a "usage" folder might be something like "Business Travel Essentials," meaning apps you use only when traveling for business._

10

What to Delete From Your Smartphone

If you're serious about organizing your smartphone, you have to embrace the concept of deleting stuff. For various articles I've written on this topic, readers have fought back and commented that deleting content from a phone is evidence that the phone itself needs to work differently. Nay, nay, nay, I say. Learning to delete, and understanding that "deleting" certain kinds of information doesn't mean you've wiped it out of your life forever, couldn't be more important to organizing and managing a smartphone.

After reading this chapter, I hope you are downright enthusiastic to start clearing the crap off your phone. Delete apps you don't actually use or need as well as bloatware. Delete photos once you've moved them to another location. Delete music when you find songs that you don't intend to listen to this month—and more. Get ready, because we're about to launch on a deleting expedition.

For the context of this chapter, it's extremely important that we define what it means to delete.

What Does 'Delete' Mean?

Deleting content from your phone means removing it, usually because it's taking up valuable space that could be used for other things—but it does not necessarily mean you're erasing it for all time from your life. Very often, it means removing an app or music from your phone because the important stuff is already saved elsewhere and you can always reinstall it at a later date.

When you purchase apps, you are not buying "the app" so much as a license for using the app. Most people know this already, but not everyone embraces what it means. Many apps—though not all—work by asking you to sign up for an account, which becomes the keeper of all the data you put in that app. It's much less common for the app itself to actually store your information locally without also backing it up somewhere else, the major exceptions being games.

This is all to say that when you delete an app from your phone, you're not necessarily deleting your account information, and you're not even cutting yourself off from ever getting the app again (because you have a license for it and can reinstall it at any time from the store where you bought it). So for a large number of apps, deleting them is no big whoop, or at least no reason to freak out.

Reasons to Delete Smartphone Content

The main reason to delete content from your smartphone is to free up space that could be used for something else. If you have so much music on your phone that you can't download offline maps of Berlin for your trip to Germany later this year, you probably should consider taking some of that music off, at least temporarily.

The other reason to delete apps, files, photos, music, and other content from your phone is because it creates visual clutter. A messy array of apps can slow you down from doing whatever it is you initially set out to do with your phone. Visual clutter creates distractions.

I. ASSESSING SPACE

Before you go on a deleting spree, take a look at your phone's available and used space. Here's how to do it on an Android phone and an iPhone.

Android: From the home screen, go to Menu > Settings > SD card & phone storage.

You'll see an entry for SD card, which will show the total space and available (free) space for your SD card. To find the available space, look under Internal phone storage (at the bottom).

Figure 10-1: This screen shows the available and used space on an Android phone. The lowermost section shows the status of the SD card, which offers an additional block of usable space, though one is not installed on this device.

iPhone: Go to Settings > General > Usage. The storage section will show the available space on the left and the used space on the right. This page will populate with a list of all your apps and how much space they and their data eat up. It's ordered with the most space-eating apps listed highest.

Note that the iPhone reserves some space for the operating system itself, so that for a 16GB phone the total of the two will equal a little less than 16GB.

iPhone users have one more space allotment to check, and that's their iCloud account. That's discussed in more detail in Section III.

Figure 10-2: This screen shows the used and available space on an iPhone, listed at the very top. Beneath, the iPhone shows how much space is being used by each of the apps, in order from most space used to least.

The two most popular mobile phone operating systems, Android and iOS, actually have unique concerns, which I'm going to address separately.

II. ANDROID-SPECIFIC TIPS FOR DELETING CONTENT

To Remove or Not Remove Bloatware?

Before we get into the nitty-gritty of deleting apps and music you chose to put on your phone, let's take a look at removing bloatware, or data that you got whether you wanted it or not. Bloatware is more of a topic for Android users than iPhone users because iPhone users can't uninstall a lot of the apps that Apple preloads onto every phone. They're stuck with them (although iPhone users can stick unwanted Apple apps into a folder to at least get them out of sight).

Removing bloatware requires rooting your Android phone, downloading apps for assistance, freezing the bloatware apps first to ensure that removing them won't completely mess up the system, and then finally wiping them off your phone. For me, the whole process is a lot more work and risk than I think it's worth. I'd rather just ignore the apps and never use them. And that's my advice for less-experienced people: Leave the bloatware alone.

If you want to remove it, be my guest, but please proceed with caution.

If you're really gung-ho to remove bloatware, you can find instructions online for rooting your specific device and following through with the other steps that I just outlined above. But please proceed with caution if you decide to go this route.

What Belongs on the SD Card?

Keep all your documents and photos on the SD card, but not apps if you can help it. Apps benefit from the faster access speeds of on-device storage, plus they're backed up to the cloud, meaning you can re-download them if you ever have to wipe your phone.

But what if you don't know which files are on the SD card and how much space they take up? In that case, try an app called

DiskUsage, which shows files and directories on your SD card and how much space they consume. DiskUsage displays all the information graphically, making it easy to see which programs or content are eating up the most space. Just be careful when you decide to delete something you see in DiskUsage that it is what you think it is.

Organize (and Back Up!) Photos

I have yet to see an elegant solution for organizing photos on most Android devices. The problem is that it's not at all convenient to keep photos on your phone. They pile up quickly and eat up a good deal of space. Plus, organizing them to any real degree on a phone is practically impossible.

So firstly, store your photos on the SD card. How you set up your phone to do that will vary based on what device you own, but many offer the option from the camera app's settings. Open the camera app and click the gear icon, then scroll down to the very bottom. If the storage option is gray, it means you don't have an SD card installed or your phone is not recognizing the one you do have installed (in which case, eject it and remount it). If you don't see the option in the camera app, you might also have to look Settings > Storage.

Second, if you can take a few minutes to move photos off of your Android phone or SD card to your computer or into a cloud storage solution, do so because it's the best and fastest way to free up some space and start organizing your photos. Keep a couple of pictures of your friends and pets on your phone if you want, but delete the majority of the images once you've transferred them to your computer. (And then back them up to yet another location!)

Third, put a backup solution in place right on your phone to ease the pressure of backing up too many photos in one shot in the future. One method would be to use Google+ and its Instant Upload feature, which automatically uploads all images from your

Android device, as you take them, to your Google+ account. A few file-syncing services, including Dropbox and SugarSync, also offer similar solutions that you can enable and that will sync your photos to the cloud in the background when you first take them. Be sure to copy those images from your file-syncing account periodically to another location (such as a computer) so that you can delete them from your phone. If you just delete them from your phone without making a copy, the file-syncing program will also delete them from its servers. (Remember, file-syncing programs are always looking to the original source for instructions on what to do with files, so deleting them from the source, your Android phone in this case, indicates the files should be deleted from the cloud, too.)

III. iPHONE-SPECIFIC TIPS FOR DELETING CONTENT

iPhone users need some specific tips for their devices, too.

What Should You Back Up in iCloud?

Apple iPhones automatically back up a lot of stuff to iCloud, the cloud-based storage and backup service that you get with an Apple device. The iCloud backup is one option for restoring your phone if you ever need to erase it and start from scratch. How much of your phone is "restored" depends on what you save in iCloud. Now, you don't have to back up to iCloud. You also have the option to back up your phone to your computer, and the advantage of doing that is that you're likely to have a lot more space for the backup. But iCloud is amazingly convenient. It's really up to you how you choose to create backups of your iPhone.

So much of what's saved to iCloud by default simply doesn't need to be there. I think it's better to maximize your iCloud space for the very important data that you'll want to back up, so here's how to figure out what you can delete.

On the same Usage screen where you found your available and used space (Settings > General > Usage), scroll down to the iCloud section, and you'll find total and available storage listed.

Figure 10-3: This screen on iPhone shows total and available storage space in your iCloud account.

Free iCloud accounts get 5GB of storage. Click Manage Storage to delete some of what's kept in iCloud. You'll see a list of apps that you can toggle on and off (on to back up to iCloud, off to delete it from iCloud).

Figure 10-4: On an iPhone, you can go to Settings > iCloud > Storage &
Backup > Manage Storage, choose your device, and then select which
apps will be backed up to iCloud. (This list can also be found by going to
Settings > General > Usage > iCloud Manage Storage and selecting your
device.)

As I mentioned, when you have an app that runs off an account
kept in the cloud, you don't necessarily have to back up data from
that app into iCloud. You will, however, want to back up an app to
iCloud if you have some complicated settings and customizations
configured for that app that, were you to lose them, would result
in a lot of time and effort to replicate. And again, games are a big
exception. Your saved game state (levels completed and such) and
other game attributes are not usually saved to an account. They're
more likely to be part of the app, and if you want to keep them,
you should back them up to iCloud.

To give an example, I just looked through my iCloud backup
and turned off backups for the travel apps Kayak and Kayak Pro.

There isn't anything about the Kayak apps and how they're installed on my phone that I need backed up. I still have that license to reinstall the apps, both the free one and the 99-cent Pro version, and all my Kayak information is stored with Kayak in my Kayak account. So there really is no need to back up that data to iCloud. Delete! On the other hand, my Podcast app contains a lot of customizations, like the order in which I list shows and which episodes are marked played, so I do want to backup that data to iCloud.

IV. PHOTOS

Why do mobile phone platforms make it so difficult to intelligently name and tag images so that you can categorize and sort them better? If I think too much about all the features that stock photo apps lack, it makes me batty. You're doing yourself a disservice if you keep all your photos on your phone for that very reason—lack of ability to name, tag, and sort them. Move your photos to your computer or automatically upload them to a cloud-based service (or both), and then delete the ones you don't need to reference from your phone.

Sure, you should save a couple of pictures of your kids, pets, most recent vacation, and other meaningful photos, but really important visual material should not be stored in the stock photo app. The reason? It's so hard to find there.

A much better place to store important images that you might need to search to find (like photos of whiteboards and other visuals from meetings) is Evernote. It makes all your images searchable, and you can add tags, notes, geo-location data, and other information that matters. Another example of images that are better kept in Evernote than in the stock photo app: damage to your home or building if, say, a storm wreaked havoc on your neighborhood and you need these images for insurance purposes. If the photos are in Evernote, you can keep other important information about the storm, insurance claim, and other details all in one place.

Even better, the photos won't be saved locally on your phone, unless you have an Evernote Premium account and set up an offline notebook. So you get the benefit of adding metadata, searchability, syncing, and the photos aren't taking up space on your smartphone. It's really quite brilliant.

Monthly checklist: Once a month or so, it's a good idea to flick through the photo albums on your phone and delete images that you know are backed up elsewhere. Put off this task for too long, and it becomes much harder to complete.

V. MUSIC, VIDEOS, PODCASTS AND GAMES

When you check your available storage space, you'll see the apps taking up the most space at the top. Usually, the worst space-eating offenders are media apps: music, videos, podcasts, games, ebooks, and magazines.

Music

People who are heavily into music usually want, deep down in their hearts, to carry their complete music collection with them wherever they go. That's simply impractical and foolish. A better system is to rotate through your collection based on what you want to hear once a week or once a month.

Monthly checklist: Make it part of your weekly or monthly routine to rotate the music you keep on your phone, meaning remove some playlists and albums and replace them with new ones. After doing it a few times, you might actually start to look forward to the task. It will give you a moment in your week or month when you stop and appreciate your music collection, flip through old albums you haven't played in ages, make decisions about what you will load onto your phone and delete from it.

Videos

If you think music takes up a lot of space, wait till you get a load of videos.

My take on videos, like movies and television shows, is to only keep on your phone those you intend to watch in the next few days or weeks. Load them up before a flight, for example, and then remove them after you've finished watching them

For short videos that you've recorded with your phone, transfer them onto your computer as soon as possible, or upload them to YouTube or another video hosting site. Note that you can mark YouTube content as private. The sooner you transfer these files to another location, the sooner you can free up the space they're consuming.

Podcasts

As with videos, I delete podcasts as soon as I'm done listening to them. If I find an episode that I just love and might want to listen to again, I might save it, but everything else is deleted the moment the show is over. Deleting the content as soon as you've finished it is by far the easiest way to keep up with this clean-up task.

Games

Games can also take up huge amounts of space on your phone. The one tricky thing to remember about games is that if you delete them, you'll likely also be deleting your saved game state, leaderboard standings, and other data. If the game is one that has an end and you've completed it, you may be ready to wipe that puppy off your phone. For other games, it all depends on how near and dear to your heart they are. As much as I love games, I'm not sentimental about them enough to hoard them on my phone. When I've lost interest or completed the game, I delete it.

Ebooks and Magazines

I would recommend keeping books you are currently reading on your phone, plus reference material that you actually use, and perhaps one more book that you have lined up next (in case you finish one title and want to start the next one immediately). With ebooks, it's generally pretty simple to delete them and re-download them as necessary.

The same goes for magazines. Keep current ones that you're reading on your device, and do your best to delete others. For monthly magazines, you might want to implement a rule for yourself of deleting any issues that are more than three months old.

VI. ODDS AND ENDS AND APPS

Focusing on deleting media first will result in real payoffs. You'll see big chunks of space free up on your phone. But there's so much more you can delete to clear up that visual clutter, even if it only takes up a nominal amount of your phone's storage.

Texts and Call History

If you're on a real cleaning spree, delete old texts and your call history. Most text-messaging apps have features and tools that let you wipe out all texts, texts from certain people, and other slices of your entire text-messaging history. The same goes for your call history.

Cache and Browser History

Monthly checklist: Clear your cache and browser history. You should routinely do this chore, maybe once a month or so. It's very easy to forget to do it. The cache essentially keeps data on hand (like Web images) to help make your browser load pages faster, but the stuff in it can quickly add up, and it's not useful to keep data for pages that you may never load ever again. Some people also see clearing the cache and browser history as a security measure, too, as you might not want a miscreant who gets his hands on your phone to be able to see where you've been on the Internet.

Apps

Every so often, I like to browse through all my apps and take a moment to remove any that I just simply don't use. You can do this while you're rearranging apps (see the Additional Content in the previous chapter), or any time you have a few minutes to kill. If you're going to delete an app that you truly do not use, just chuck it and forget about it. If you're not sure whether you have anything important in the app and need more time to review it, move it into a folder labeled "To Delete" and review it when you can.

The Do-Over

If all else fails and your phone is a complete disaster, back up your important data, and then do a factory reset. The factory reset button in the Settings will wipe your phone and give you a complete "do-over" status. It's not a bad option, even though a lot of people may be scared of what it can do. If you keep most of your files, photos, and even some app settings in the cloud, you might not need more than a half hour to re-set up your phone from scratch, this time only loading onto it what you need, and forgetting about the junk that previously made it a mess in the first place.

The last time I upgraded my phone, that's exactly what I did. I started with a blank slate and only downloaded onto it apps that I thought I might need. I could see from my list of "Purchased" apps that, over the years, I had downloaded dozens and dozens that I never used. I didn't even recognize a good number of them. Your phone doesn't have to be "perfect" and contain every app you might ever need. You can always add more later.

VII. TAKE-AWAYS

- Deleting content from your smartphone doesn't mean erasing it permanently, as you can very often restore apps and their data.
- Deleting content frees up memory/space on your phone and helps eliminate visual clutter, which can be distracting.
- Media content, such as photos, videos, music, and podcasts, typically take up the most space, meaning you'll get back an optimized amount of space if you delete them, or at least temporarily remove them when you're not enjoying them. Cycle through your media by regularly adding and removing what tickles your fancy to reduce the amount of space they consume.
- Game apps don't always back up to the cloud, so only remove them when you are sure you're finished with them and don't want to save your game state, leaderboard stats, and so forth.

- Additional Content -

How to Merge Contacts on an Android Phone

Do you have duplicate contacts in your phone's address book? The first way to clean them up is to use a computer to log in to the

Google account that's affiliated with your phone and go to con-
tacts.google.com.

Along the left side, choose a group of contacts, like My Contacts
Most Contacted, etc. Under the More button, choose Find &
merge duplicates.

Easy, right? You can repeat this process by searching for a specific name (I found duplicates of myself when searching for "Jill"
for example) or by selecting different groups from the left. Be sure
to log back into your phone and refresh using the Sync Now button in the Settings when you're done to see the changes in your
phone.

You might still see duplicate contacts as a result of syncing contacts from other sources, such as Facebook. You can suppress or
remove those accounts if you don't want to see them anymore.
Still, merging the contacts you have in Google could go a long way
to making your contacts list tidy.

IV

Part IV: Personal

11

Photos

The disorganization problems most people have with their photos comes from the fact that they can take so many photos so easily and have dozens of excellent options for sharing them. In other words, it's a high-class problem to have. Compared with film photography, digital photography is amazingly convenient and inexpensive. Start-up costs aside, like the price of a camera, memory card, and computer, it's basically free. Digital cameras let photo enthusiasts, amateurs, and even the worst photographers become highly prolific.

If you have a disastrously messy photo collection, it probably didn't happen overnight, but rather over many years of taking photos with various devices and sharing them via websites that were popular at the time. There may have been a few years when you snapped a few thousand photos with a point-and-shoot camera and then uploaded them to Flickr. And then maybe you realized that more people who wanted to see your pictures were hanging out on Facebook, so you started uploading dozens of photos you snapped with your iPhone or Android to that site. Oh, and let's not forget about all those images you shot with your D-SLR and transferred to your computer, but never really put anywhere else.

Before you dive deeply into this chapter, I want you to consider for a moment one option regarding how to organize your photos—and I fully know that a lot of people will reject the idea, but hear me out. Rather than organize your entire photo collection, consider just putting in place a workflow and system of organizing them moving forward. In other words, forget about everything you have and only think about future photos.

This advice is similar to a recommendation I gave in Chapter 1 about "sweeping" old files into year folders. If you recall, the gist of it is to lump together all the old files you have into folders labeled by year (such as "2009" and "2010"), and then promptly forget about them so you can focus on the new files and folders you'll create going forward. You're not deleting anything. You're not making any of your data less searchable than it was before. And most importantly, you're not getting caught up in a pointless task of organizing for organization's sake.

Now, some people will rail against this advice for their photos (even more people reject the idea for their music, which is why I don't even suggest it in Chapter 12), but here are the facts:

- Your photos are a mess.
- Cleaning them up and organizing them is really hard work.
- Organizing old photos is horrendously time-consuming.
- If you spend all your time and energy trying to clean up the backlog of image files, you'll ignore the new incoming photos that you are continuing to take, which compound the existing problem.
- Ask yourself honestly, "To what end will I be organizing my old photos?" What will the payoff be, and how much of it will you actually see? If you only go into your old photos once or twice a year to find an image, is the payoff of doing that task slightly quicker going to be sufficient to warrant the massive task you will undertake by cleaning up the old collection?

In many cases, it simply makes sense to forget about the backlog of data and focus on creating a workflow that you can use from this day forward to keep new photos well organized, searchable, shareable, and backed up. Only after you have a system in place for processing new images should you spend time condensing your older, disparate photo collections and reorganizing them in a way that suits your needs.

This chapter will first cover a bit of very basic photography software vocabulary. Feel free to simply skim or skip that section if you're already familiar with the terminology. Note that it doesn't cover the vocabulary of cameras, but just a few words related to the software side that I want to be sure are clear. Second, I'll walk you through the process of creating a new workflow for organizing your photos. Third, I'll explore some options for dealing with the backlog of photo data that is probably scattered across a dozen different devices and websites (and as I said before, you may very well just skip this part and live with your old photos being a little messy, as it might be more of a waste of your time to change it). And finally, I'll leave you with a summary of take-aways and a list of tools and services for organizing and sharing your photos.

I. BASICE PHOTO SOFTWARE VOCABULARY

Exif data

Exif stands for exchangeable image file format. It's a standard used for images and sound files, but all you really need to know for this chapter is that "Exif data" on an image file means metadata. Your camera automatically records Exif data every time you snap a picture. It includes the date and time the photo was taken, camera model, exposure settings, and in some cases the location where the photo was shot.

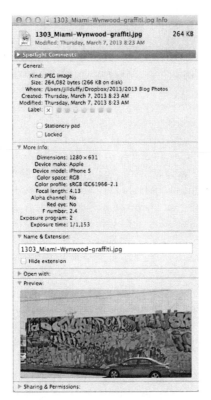

Figure 11-1. Exif data shows you additional metadata about any image on your computer.

Tip:

To see Exif data for an image in Windows,
select the image file in Windows Explorer,
and look at the bottom of the window.
Drag the top edge of this area up to enlarge

it, and more information will appear. Or
right-click on a photo file in Windows
Explorer and choose Properties > Details
to find the Exif information. On a Mac,
just right-click (Command-click) any
image file and select Get Info. You can
toggle open the different panes, and the
majority of the Exif data will be in the
section called More Info.

Facial Detection, Facial Recognition, or Face-tagging

Face-tagging means tagging someone's actual face in an image
with his or her name. For face-tagging to be useful beyond ordi-
nary tagging, it needs to also use face-detection and facial-recog-
nition features. Face detection means the software can detect that
there is a face in the image, whereas facial recognition means the
software is guessing whose face it is. The more often you face-
tag "Jill Duffy," the better the software gets at guessing when new
photos of Jill Duffy are imported.

Geo-tagging or Geolocation information

Geolocation information is exactly what it sounds like: data telling
where you were when you took a photo. Some cameras support
geo-tagging, and you'll always find it as an option in modern
smartphone cameras either natively or via an app that will add it
to your images. Photography software often adds a picture of a
map, as well as the city, state or province, and country name, so
it's much more than just GPS coordinates.

Importing vs. Transferring

There's a difference between "importing" photos and merely "transferring" or copying them from your camera or smartphone to your computer. Transferring or copying image files simply means you move them from the camera to the computer, leaving you with the ability to do little more than rename the files and group them into folders. Importing, on the other hand, lets you add more information to the photos and often can automatically rename the images according to some rules you set, for example, renaming all imported images in a session with a few descriptive words followed by a sequence of numbers, like "2013_Argentina (1 of 99)." When importing, you can also add tags, descriptions, captions, and so forth.

II. CREATING A WORKFLOW FOR ORGANIZING NEW PHOTOS

Taking a few simple steps to properly name, group, and tag your photos at the time of import will end up saving you huge amounts of time later when you start to hunt through your images looking for the pictures you want to share, print, or use in a project. Here are the steps I recommend.

Step 1. Import Photos

The first thing to address is which application you'll use to import images from your camera or phone. Mac users can choose iPhoto as their default because it comes preinstalled on most Apple computers, and Windows users can use Windows Live Photo Gallery for the same reason. If you want to use a more sophisticated piece of software, by all means do. See the list of recommended software and tools at the end of this chapter.

Tip:

Don't use the software that comes with
your camera to import photos. It rarely
if ever has the best selection of editing
and importing tools, and in most cases,
your computer will come with free
software already installed that's better.
Or, you can buy specialty photography
software if you want the super-duper
package.

Regardless of which application you use to import your photos, take a moment to explore the options that are available in the settings. Most programs use a default by-date setting to group your images, meaning it will recommend sets based on the dates when the photos were shot, which is good! It's especially helpful when the software also creates a folder for the group that uses a date in the folder name. You can always change the settings or change the folder names. But it usually makes sense to keep dates in the name of the folders because it makes them easier to find, search, and sort. I'm a big believer in finding information by date, and that's especially true with photos.

Step 2. Organize Photos Into Sets or Albums

While you're still sitting in front of your computer, right after you finish importing images, take a few moments to organize your photos into sets or albums, and name them something descriptive. Most people think about their photos as they relate to an event or a date—and even when it's an event, that event is tied to a date.

For example, you'll remember "Peter's graduation" took place in "May 2010." Use those primary descriptive words and dates in the set or album name.

Figure 11-2. People tend to remember photos based on an event that happened when the photo was taken. Photography software generally encourages you to organize photos into groups that are labeled by the event name.

Tip:

Think of organizing photos into sets or albums as part of the importing process. That way, you won't do step 1 and stop. You'll instead get into the habit of always setting up albums and sets every time you import new images, and that will help you keep your photo organization efforts on track.

Step 3. Name the Files and Lightly Edit Them

The next step is to rename the photo files and lightly edit them. I quickly look through my photos one by one and take a moment to rename them, and maybe do a little bit of cleanup work, such as cropping the image or rotating it. I don't get caught up in retouching and messing with the color levels and such at this stage, however. Save that for later when you want to do something with the photos.

Not everyone agrees with me that renaming photo files is worth their time, especially if the photos have other data, such as ratings or "favorite" markers and face tags. But because of the way I tend to look for information, often scanning lists of files via the operating system's folder view, I get tremendous value out of having a clear file-naming convention, which I already fully outlined in Chapter 2, and for photos, it's not much different.

Here's how I name my photo files.

I start with a six-digit date representing year, month, and day, such that 120105 means January 5, 2012. If you forget the full date, you can find it in the Exif, and when all else fails, a four-digit year and month are good enough.

Next, I add a second identifier (the date is the first identifier). This second identifier tells me something more about the photo, and I often use shorthand codes for it. "NYC" might be pictures from a trip to New York City. One abbreviation I use a lot is "bg" for photos that I specifically shot for my blog. Your second identifier can be anything that makes sense to you: the location, something about the event, a family name, and so on.

Adding a third or fourth identifier will depend on how much time you have. If I'm in a rush to I'll simply use a number, for example:

- 120105_ski_01
- 120105_ski_02

Looking at those filenames, I would know these images were from a ski trip on January 5, 2012. If I have time, I'll end the filename with something more specific than a number, such as the name of the person or another keyword that describes the image:

- 120105_ski_lodge
- 120105_ski_Mom-jump
- 120105_ski_fireside

See how quickly it all comes together? You can now tell just by the filename what is in the photo and when it was taken. Knowing this information will save you a lot of time later when you want to find images or upload them to another location in bulk.

As you go through the images to rename them, you should also lightly edit them, by which I mean weed out the duds, like blurry photos or the worst shot of a set of five that are virtually identical. During this step is also a convenient time to quickly blast off any red eyes or other obvious flaws that don't require a lot of focus and time to fix. Better to do it now and get it out of the way than forget and share an ugly photo accidentally later.

Step 4. Add More Data

If you're taking the time to go through your images one by one to rename them, you might as well add more data to them, including tags, descriptions or captions, and ratings. I personally skip over this step at the time of import because I don't really use the extra data so much to find and organize my pictures. If you do use it, though, include this step here as part of your importing and organizing workflow.

Note that the additional information you add to the photos in this step may be lost if you upload the images later to another platform. Facebook is notorious for not bringing photo data along with it. Still, it's not a bad idea to write descriptions while they're fresh in your mind. You can always copy and paste them into another platform later.

Step 5. Back Up!

With your photos imported and pretty well organized, be sure they are backed up! Hopefully you've read Chapter 6 on backing up and already have some system in place that automatically backs up your entire computer. If you use some wonky manual system, do whatever it is you need to do (like copy the files to another location) now before you get any further.

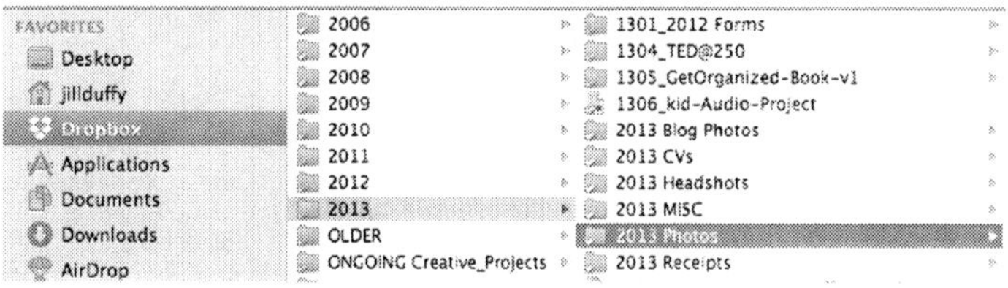

Figure 11-3. Saving photos to a Dropbox or other file-syncing account helps make them accessible and shareable, while also backing them up.

Step 6. Add the Photos to a Secondary, Shareable Location

I think a great way to make a secondary backup of your photos is to put them into a service that lets you share them easily. To share them is a big reason many of us take photos in the first place. Facebook and Flickr are fine choices. File-syncing programs, such as Dropbox and SugarSync, are better for people who prefer to keep their photos private for the most part and only share them with very specific people, including those friends and family who don't have Facebook or Flickr accounts.

Tip:

A free website called ifttt (which stands for "if this, then that") lets you set up commands that automate organizational tasks and other chores related to your digital life, such as "If I post a photo to Facebook, then also save it to Dropbox." You can read more about ifttt in Chapter 13, as many of its uses relate to sites like Facebook, Twitter, Google+, and the like. But it does include some neat and handy commands for automating some of your photo organizing process, too.

III. CLEANING UP A PHOTO ARCHIVE

Once you have a new process in place, you might consider cleaning up your old photo archives, so let's get down to it.

Step 1. Locate old photos

First, you will need a list of all the places where you have photos. It could include:

- Facebook
- Flickr
- Photobucket
- SmugMug
- old computers (including different software programs, if applicable)

- old memory cards, external hard drives, or cameras
- smartphones
- iCloud Photo Stream
- Google+ Photo/Picasa
- Dropbox, Box, or another file-syncing site.

If it's been a while since you used a particular site or service, you also might need to do a password retrieval for the account (unless you use a password manager, which you should; see Chapter 5, and seriously, start using one immediately). After you've figured out where your photos are stored and have unlocked all the accounts, you then need to see whether each account offers a simple export option for moving all your photos to a new place. For example, Facebook does have an option that lets you download all your photos, although it isn't exactly simple or quick. See the Additional Content for complete details on how to download your Facebook photos.

Step 2. Create a Spreadsheet

Assuming you have photos in more than three or four places, create a simple spreadsheet so you keep track of all the places where you find photos. You'll have a column indicating the location of the photos, another perhaps marking its priority level (if you know there are certain photos you want sooner than others), another indicating whether it offers a simple export option (hint: Mark Facebook as "no" for this column), and one to check off whether you've completed the transfer of files. That final column is the most important one because it could take days or weeks to get through all of them, and you wouldn't want to unnecessarily repeat any work you've already done.

This spreadsheet could also tip you off as to where you want to start putting all the photo files you have. Keep notes on the different sites and services as you use them. Hopefully one that you're already using is one that you want to continue using for all your images moving forward.

Step 3. Compile Your Images

Decide on the primary and secondary locations where you'll store your photos. If you're totally lost, I recommend using your computer as the primary location, saved to a folder that syncs, such as a Dropbox folder. Dropbox is now your secondary location. Done.

You can begin exporting photos from the old locations and importing them into the new ones. Note that Facebook has such a convoluted and involved process for extracting and downloading your data that you'll want to factor in at least two days for it. I'm not kidding.

Take your time, track your progress in the spreadsheet, and know that this is a long project that requires a bit of dedication to see through to the end. You may lose additional data, like captions and face-tags as you transfer files between services. It's up to you if you want to copy and paste the information that gets lost along the way, but if you are planning to do it, do it now while the photos and context of the additional data are still fresh in your mind.

Step 4. Automate for the Future

If at all possible, you'll want to put automations in place so that your photos go to your new desired locations automatically in the future. For example, you can turn on the "automatic upload" feature on an Android phone to always have your photos copied into Google+ Photos. There's a similar feature for SugarSync's mobile app as well as Dropbox's mobile app that saves all pictures that you take into your file-syncing account. If you have an iPhone and iPhoto on a Mac, you can turn on Photo Stream to always have photos from both places show up on the other.

Depending on what products and services you use, this could be quite simple or extremely difficult, which is why I recommended taking notes on all the different services on your spreadsheet. It will serve as a powerful source of information as you decide where and how to host your photos.

IV. TAKE-AWAYS

- Organizing a photo collection is arduous work, and you should really consider what the payoff will be before undertaking such a task to make sure it's worth your while.
- Putting in place a workflow or system for importing images will ensure you are no longer adding to the disorganized pile of images you already have. In other words, at least all your new images from this day forth will be organized.
- Use filenames, set or albums, tags, and other metadata to help you organize your photos. Often the goal of organizing a photo collection is being able to find an image, and the metadata lets you do just that.
- If you do decide to organize a backlog of photo files, work systematically and use a spreadsheet to keep track of your progress.
- Save all your images into two locations: a primary location for storage (which should be backed up) and a secondary location where you can easily share the photos. See the Additional Content at the end of this chapter for advice on sharing.

V. RECOMMENDED SOFTWARE AND SERVICES

Photography Editing and Organizing Software

- ACDSee or ACDSee Pro (professional level)
- Adobe Bridge (for workflow management only)
- Adobe Photoshop (professional level; for editing only)
- Adobe Photoshop Elements (enthusiast level)
- Adobe Photoshop Express iPad App (entry level)
- Adobe Photoshop Lightroom (professional level)
- Aperture (professional level)
- Corel AfterShot Pro (professional level)
- Corel PaintShop Photo Pro (enthusiast level)
- CyberLink PhotoDirector (professional level)
- iPhoto (entry level; comes included with most Apple computers)
- Mac OS X's Image Capture (entry level)
- Nero Kwik Media (entry level)
- Picasa (entry level)
- Serif PhotoPlus
- Shotwell
- Windows Live Photo Gallery (entry level; comes free on most Windows computers)
- Windows 7's Import Pictures (entry level)
- Windows 8's Photos app (entry level)

Image Hosting Services

- 500px
- Adobe Revel

- Apple iCloud Photo Stream
- Flickr
- Picasa Web Albums
- SmugMug

-

- Additional Content -

Tips for Sharing Photo Collections

When you organize groups of digital photos into collections (sometimes also called albums or sets), think about who is going to view them and in what context. In all likelihood, you won't be sitting side-by-side with Uncle Artie while he's looking at pictures of the kids. Help him understand what he's seeing.

Collection names. The name of a photo collection will probably be similar to, or at least reflective of, the secondary identifier in your filename. And if you've used a secondary identifier—ta-da!—the collections are already sorted for you.

Be sure the collection name is descriptive but also enticing. If you want your friends and family to actually look at the photos, the collection name needs to draw them in the same way a good headline attracts you to read an article. "Family Winter Vacation" is fine, but "Pocono Ski Trip" may be better. "Grandma's First Ski Jump" might be even better.

Captions. Do write captions for your images. Don't assume that people know what they are seeing. Include names of people and the location at the very least. With some cameras, software, and photo-sharing sites, facial recognition features and geo-location tags will add this information for you automatically.

How many images to share? Just because a digital camera lets you take 1,000 shots in one day doesn't mean you should share them all. Pick only the best images, and try to not to post too many duplicates when sharing your photos.

Everyone has his or her own tolerance for how many photos they're willing to view in one sitting. I max out somewhere between 40 and 75, depending on the type of images and how familiar I am with the people and setting. Use your judgment in deciding how many images to share in a set. If you feel you're pushing the limit with the number of photos in a collection, just break it into two.

-

- Additional Content -

How to Download Your Facebook Photos

Warning: Downloading all your photos from Facebook takes longer than you might expect, although it's mostly waiting time. Give yourself two to four days to complete this project.

1. Go to your Account Settings in Facebook (gear icon in the top right).

2. On the left side, select General. You'll see a list of choices, and below them, in a totally different font, you'll see a link to Download your data. Select it.

3. Click on "Download a copy of your Facebook data" and click through the next few prompts asking to start your archive and whatnot.

4. Check your email for a confirmation message. You'll now likely have to wait a little while, perhaps half an hour, or as long as a day or two, until you get another message saying the archive has been created and is ready for you to download.

The finished archive contains much more than just your photos. There's no way to download only photos, but at least the pictures are all collected into one folder called Photos. You'll have to go through the subfolders to decipher what's in them, but you can pretty quickly match them to the albums you have online. My advice would be to rename the folders, but not the image files, to help guide you through what's what.

12

Music

Duplicate tracks, unnamed albums, a disarray of miscellaneous songs and audio files—if those words describe your digital music collection, there are a number of ways you can better organize it, and I'll explain them in this chapter.

I'm focusing on iTunes specifically, as it is the most popular software for managing music today. It also covers other aspects of music management, such as strategies for creating backups, and includes some recommendations for storage devices and services.

People who have very large music collections sometimes refer to themselves as digital music hoarders. If you're a hoarder, it's extremely important that you read the first section in this chapter. Anytime you clean up or reorganize almost anything, you need to be prepared to clear out some clutter. I know a lot of digital music hoarders are absolutely unwilling to delete anything from their music collections (that's why it's a "collection"). That's fine, but if you intend to keep everything, you need to have realistic expectations and goals for your clean-up project. I'll try to walk you through some of those realities.

My strategy for cleaning up iTunes relies heavily on the tools iTunes provides—not third-party cleaning apps, although they do exist and in some cases, you may want to use them. A few are listed at the end of the chapter. One reason you might not want a third-party app is because you want to keep a watchful eye on what's happening to your files during the process and maintain control of your library.

The steps outlined in this chapter will help improve your library and solve some common problems many people encounter while managing their music collections. It's time-consuming and difficult to fix every problem with every song or track, so have patience while you're undertaking this project. Because it's such a massive job, the best way to fix a music collection in my mind is bit by bit, rather than all at once.

I. WHAT IS YOUR GOAL?

You might recall from the Introduction and Chapter 1 my whole rigmarole about needing clear goals for your organizational ventures, as well as understanding that you don't need to be perfect or have a "perfectly" organized system for anything.

Music collectors often imagine they want a perfectly organized library, a system in which all their files are appropriately tagged, labeled, sorted, and so forth.

But to what end?

I'm asking you to ask yourself that question seriously. What is the purpose of having a perfectly organized music library? What will you do with it then that you can't do now? What do you want to be able to do?

If the answer is you want things neatly labeled and organized so they can be "correct," then you're wasting your time. That's organization for organization's sake, with no clear desired outcome.

If, on the other hand, you want to remove duplicates of songs so that you can free up space on your hard drive, or you want to label songs that are currently unlabeled or mislabeled so that you can better find them, sort them, arrange them into playlists, and actually listen to them (all excellent reasons to clean up a music collection), then we're in business. Again, what do you want to do with your music collection? I can't stress enough how important it is to answer that question before you start.

Estimated time: Depending on the size and current state of your music collection, plus your goals, this project could take anywhere from 1 hour to 10 hours or more, in which case you should break it up into 1-hour tasks across several weeks. I recommend setting aside about an hour on a weekend to begin. You'll use that initial hour to:

- set your goals
- create a plan for your cleanup process
- if there's time left over, begin putting the plan into action.

Tip:

Set aside an hour or two across a couple of weekends to continue cleaning up your music. Trying to do it all at once will be stressful and frustrating. I've outlined the steps in this chapter such that you can easily break them up into a series of smaller projects.

II. WHERE ARE YOUR MUSIC FILES?

When you upload or download music, albums, podcasts, etc., through iTunes, the software puts those files and other data related to them into a very specific place by default:

- Windows 7 and 8: C:\Users\username\My Music\ iTunes\

- Windows Vista: C:\Users\username\Music\iTunes\
- Windows XP: C:\Documents and Settings\username\
  My Documents\My Music\iTunes\
- Mac OS X: /Users/username/Music/iTunes/

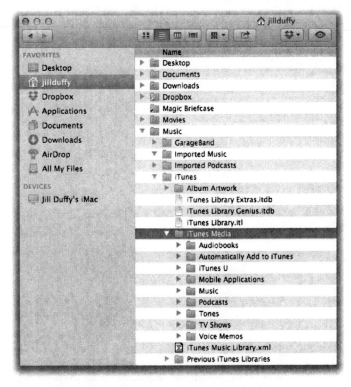

Figure 12-1: iTunes places your music files into a folder for iTunes Media by default.

If you move your files or change that default location, iTunes can become very confused about your music collection, which can be a huge source of frustration and the reason you feel like your collection is disorganized. But there are a number of reasons you might want to change the location. Here are three basic options for choosing the file location. Option 1 explains why you might use the default location, while options 2 and 3 take into account two possible reasons you might change it.

Option 1: Use the Default Location, Period

If you've never run into space constraints because of the size of your music collection, I would keep it simple and leave your music in the default location that iTunes has set up. This solution is amazingly straightforward, doesn't require any work on your behalf, and won't create any snags when you upgrade to a new computer and transfer all your files from the old machine to the new one.

Option 2: Move All Your Files to a New Location

If your music collection eats up a lot of space and you want to move it to, say, an external hard drive or another computer so that you can free up space on your primary computer, you have to first make sure you'll preserve the iTunes data when you move your files, and then remap iTunes so it knows to now look for your files in their new location.

Note that in this example, you would be moving your entire collection to the new location. In other words, you'll be playing your music from the external hard drive, which means you'll need to have that hard drive connected to your computer any time you listen to music. Don't confuse this option with moving some of your music to a hard drive to set it aside for the time being. I'll cover that strategy as the third option.

Here's how to move your entire collection and remap iTunes.

Step 1: Connect the storage device or network the secondary computer to the primary one, if you're moving your music off your primary computer. (You would skip this step if you're moving the collection to a separate partition of your primary computer.)

Step 2: Choose to keep iTunes media organized.

- Launch iTunes.
- Open Preferences (Windows users will find it under "Edit," and Mac users will find it until the "iTunes" menu).
- Go to the Advanced tab.
- Make sure the box next to "Keep iTunes Media folder organized" is checked.
- Click OK.

This selection preserves any existing organization on your music files, such as sorting songs into album and artist folders, and other metadata. I'll explain more about metadata a little later.

Step 3: Remap iTunes' default location. Stay in the Window for Advance settings and then:

- You'll see a section at the top for iTunes Media folder location; click Change.
- Navigate to the location where you want to keep your music collection. Remember, if you're using an external device, it needs to be connected and switched on.
- Choose to make a new folder and type in the name of the folder, such as "External iTunes Media" or something else that's easily identifiable to you.
- Confirm by selecting either OK or Create, depending on your version of iTunes.
- Click OK in the Advanced settings window.

- Go to File > Library > Organize Library (in older versions of iTunes, it may say "Consolidate Library"). If you see an additional option to "consolidate library," check that box.
- Click OK. All your music and media files will now be sent to the new location. There must be enough space available to copy all your music and media files. See the Additional Content at the end of this chapter for how to check how much space you will need.
- After the folder has been copied, locate your original iTunes Media folder, and drag it to the trash or recycle bin, but do not delete the iTunes Library files that may be in that same location. Those are the files containing your playlists and such. Just to be safe, do not yet empty the trash.

Step 4: Quit iTunes and re-launch it. If you see an error message, it probably means you deleted the iTunes Library files, so pick them out of the trash and put them back into the default location.

Option 3: Move Some, But Not All, of Your Music

The third and final option looks something like this: You want to continue using iTunes with all the default settings, but you have so much music that your computer runs slowly because of all the space it takes up. So you'll create a backup of some files so that you can delete them from iTunes, while leaving a good chunk of music, podcasts, audiobooks, and whatnot in the default location.

There are many ways you can back up some—but not all—of your music. You could burn albums to discs, move files to a USB drive, keep the music on an old computer, create a backup copy using an online backup service—the sky's the limit. Chapter 6 contains more details about creating backups. And remember that the most important rule of backing up is to have at least two copies of your data, but preferably three.

If your music is already organized in such a fashion that you know what you want to remove, perhaps based on album or artist, then copying over the files and deleting them from iTunes is a snap. If it's not, however, you probably want to continue reading the rest of this chapter first, and come back to this section at the end.

How to copy files onto a drive and remove them from iTunes and your computer: Here's the easiest way to make a copy of your files and then remove them from iTunes to free up space:

- Connect your backup device or service.
- Open the default location of your iTunes Media folder.
- Select the folders that contain the music you want to backup.
- Drag them onto the new device and wait until they finish copying.

Optional: I would then disconnect the device, reconnect it, and check to be sure the files aren't corrupt by attempting to play two or three of them at random.

Then you can delete the music by simply dragging the appropriate folders form the default location into the trash.

Figure 12-2: Copying music files to a new location may be a good idea if you need to free up space on your computer.

How to copy ("burn") files onto CDs or DVDs and remove them from iTunes and your computer: There's a second method for creating backups that you can perform entirely in iTunes itself. This method is limited to CDs (audio, MP3, and data CDs) and DVDs. One problem with this method is that deleting the songs may take additional time and effort, depending on how sloppy your library has become. Here's how to do it:

- Put all the songs you want to back up and remove into a playlist. I recommend creating one playlist called something like "To Backup."
- From the album or artist view, you can simply right-click on a selection to create a playlist that includes all the songs in that album or by that artist.
- Once you have a playlist of files to backup, right-click on it and select Burn playlist to disc.
- Choose the format and other options you want. Burn the disc. Eject the disc when it's finished.

Optional: Reinsert the disc and spot-check that the files aren't corrupt by attempting to play two or three files at random.

The last step is to delete the songs from iTunes, and it's a little complicated, but there's a trick to make it simpler. If the music you burned comprises, say, one complete album, you can just sort you music by album and select to delete all the songs in that album. On the other hand, if the music came from a jumble of artists and albums, it's a pain in the neck. One little hack is to intentionally enter incorrect metadata (more about metadata in the next section) to make it easy to group all the files together. For example, select all the songs in question; right-click and choose Get Info; and then enter some false information into the metadata, like "Album: Songs to Delete" so that you can now sort by "album" and find all these songs to delete.

III. HOW TO IDENTIFY UKNOWN TRACKS AND FILL IN METADATA AND ALBUM ARTWORK IN iTUNES

What do you do if you have a whole bunch of songs that have no title, no artist, and no album name? Or what about songs that have only some of that information but are missing others? You need to get the metadata.

Filling in metadata can make an enormous dent in your efforts to clean up your music library. Metadata is the information about a song, such as its title, the artist who performed it, the artist who wrote or composed it, its album name, the artwork from the album cover, the year it was released, and so forth. When you have correct metadata, you can sort and search for your files with greater ease, and that's huge.

Figure 12-3: Metadata in iTunes helps you sort and manage your music more efficiently.

If your music library contains a lot of music that you originally ripped from CDs, getting metadata will be supremely easy because, as long as you're connected to the Internet, iTunes can do it automatically for you by comparing your songs to more than a billion that are stored in Gracenote's compact disc database (CCDB).

Gracenote has partnered with Apple to put this toolkit at your fingertips in iTunes. CDDB stores information and metadata about music. With iTunes' help, it can automatically find and fill in missing information for miscellaneous and unlabeled music in your iTunes library. It can't fix everything in your music library, but it can reorganize and correct a ton of bad or missing information very quickly.

Getting metadata from Gracenote only works reliably if your music came from discs imported through iTunes. If you have a ton of bootleg music or tracks downloaded from other sources, your success rate will vary.

Note that album artwork is treated slightly differently, so it's handled separately in the instructions that follow.

Here's how to get the metadata automatically:

1. Connect to the Internet
You have to be connected to the Internet for this to work.

2. Select the Tracks
Select the tracks for which you're missing the track name, album title, artist, or any other metadata—but don't select tracks which are only missing album artwork. You'll work most efficiently if you get the metadata first and album artwork after. (To select multiple tracks at a time, highlight the first track, hold Shift, and select the last one.)

Tip:

Select no more than about 20 tracks
at a time so you can spot-check whether
they update correctly.

---

3. Get Metadata
Either from the Advanced tab on the menu bar, or by holding control while clicking again on the block of selected tracks, choose Get Track Names.

Voilà! Repeat steps 1 through 3 for any unknown files you have.

If the metadata didn't update at all, you'll need to give iTunes a little help figuring out what files these are. In that case, you'll have to fill in a little bit of the data manually:

4. Listen to the Unknown Track

Play the unknown track and see if you can tell what it is, but don't spend a lot of time on it. As you'll see in the next few steps, you may actually wind up saving this part for later. If you have a smartphone on hand, you can use Shazam, which is a free app that identifies music. In listening to the track and trying to figure out what it is, the best metadata you can provide is probably the album name. If you can only remember the song name or artist, use the iTunes Store to your advantage to find the album. Click iTunes Store in the left rail of iTunes, and then search using the search box in the upper right for the song, artist name, or any other information that will help you identify the album name. If you can't find it at all, skip to step 5B.

5A. Update the Album Field

When you find the correct album name in the iTunes Store, go back to Music and now type it into the album field the name exactly as it appeared. Try steps 2 and 3 again and see if it now works.

5B. Shelve it for Later

If nothing has worked, put the unidentifiable song into a new playlist called something like "Unknown Tracks" or "Unknown Music" or "Songs Missing Information." You'll use this playlist to collect any songs that contain missing information so that when you have more time (remember, I recommend taking many sessions to complete this project!), you can use other methods to identify them, like playing the songs for friends.

Remember, you don't need to have a "perfect" iTunes library, and you don't want to waste too much time troubleshooting one problem when you could be getting so much more else done. Perhaps you could fill in a little information about the tracks that will help you remember what they are and create a playlist so they are grouped together so that you can tackle them later. Then, move on.

6. Optional: How to Add Missing Album Artwork

Optionally (you wouldn't want to do this if your computer is already tight on space), you can highlight any number of tracks, right-click them, and select Get Album Artwork. Within a few seconds, you should see the CD cover wherever iTunes can display it.

Figure: 12-4: You can automatically download album art in a couple of seconds for your albums in iTunes so long as Gracenote accurately identifies the albums.

You can see the album artwork by selecting Music on the left rail of iTunes and choosing the Albums view at the top.

The Problems of Downloaded Music

All the tips given so far work well for music that was imported into iTunes by disc. They don't work well for downloaded music, including tracks that were legally purchased through iTunes. So what do you do if there is missing or incorrect information for those files?

Without touching any extra tools, how could you update those files on your own? The first thing I would do is isolate those files into a playlist, or multiple playlists. Group them together so you get a sense of how much have.

You can then work on filling in the missing information in batches. Try to identify the album if you can. If you have the album name, the rest typically falls into place quickly.

Collect the information you need, or at least as much as you can, and add it to your file. I think it's easiest to type in the Info box rather than in the iTunes track listing (right-click and select Get Info).

IV. HOW TO FIND AND DELETE DUPLICATE TRACKS IN iTUNES

Now—and only now—that you've updated any missing metadata that you could, it's time to search out and eliminate duplicate tracks. If you try to take this step out of order, iTunes can misidentify titles that are not in fact duplicates but that look like duplicates based only on the metadata. If you have multiple files called Track 02 with no other information, they'll be marked as duplicates even if you can clearly see that the length of the songs are different.

1. Display Duplicates

In the menu bar, go to View and Show Duplicate Items. In older versions of iTunes, it's under File > Display Duplicates, and if you still don't see this option (if you see Display All instead), it means it's already turned on.

2. Sort the List

In my own cleanup effort, I learned not to rely on Apple's official help for this step because I noticed some idiosyncrasies with my own files, and had I followed Apple's suggestions I would have inadvertently deleted unique files. So, what worked for me was to sort the list by Name (that is, title). I then looked at the name and the length of the track to see if they matched. Some duplicates were obvious, but others seemed to be false twins. Hopefully in your own collection, you'll be able to spot some duplicates quickly.

3. Delete the Dupes

Choose a batch of duplicates to delete, but not too many at once. To work carefully, I would select no more than about 20 to 30 files at a time to delete. When you find a duplicate set, select one of the pair, and hit delete; to select multiple files at once, hold the Command or Ctrl key as you click the files that you want to delete. Once 20 to 30 of them are selected, press the delete key.

Again, as per the previous step, you want to be able to spot-check as you go so that you don't accidentally delete something that's not actually a duplicate. I think working in small batches is the best way to go about it.

V. USING PLAYLISTS TO CLEAN UP iTUNES

Once you've cleaned up most or all the music files that were originally imported using iTunes, it's time to tackle files that you pur-chased, copied, or downloaded by other means. For some music lovers, you may not have even scratched the surface yet in your cleanup project. I told you this whole thing was going to take a while. Relax. Take your time. There's no reason to rush it. My method of cleaning up these other files is to break down the pro-ject into small segments so that you are never trying to process too many files at once and so that you can do the work in batches. I'll show you how to do it in this section using Playlists in iTunes.

Step 1: Survey Your Collection

First, survey your music collection. Select "Music" from the Library menu at top left. Sort by name, first ascending then descending, and skim the list looking for any instances of music with a name field that is empty (these will sort to the very top or bottom). Look under 'U' for "unknown" and "untitled," and 'T' for "Track 01." Look for numbers where you might expect to find words. Just get a sense of what's there.

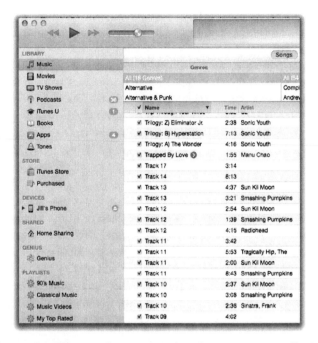

Figure 12-5: When you have unnamed tracks in your music collection, you can find them easily by sorting on the name and looking under 'T' for "Track" as well as 'U' for "Unknown."

Now sort by artist and do the same thing, and lastly by album. Have you gotten a feel for what's missing or possibly mislabeled?

You might also know the strengths and weaknesses of your music library, from an organizational standpoint, just from your experience listening every day. If that's the case, identify which weakness you're going to tackle first, such as "misnamed track titles," because you don't want to take on too much at once.

How you'll proceed at this point depends on the state of your library. You might decide that most of your collection is in good order, except that when you sorted by artist, a lot of files flagged your attention. Or you might already know that the biggest problem is mislabeled titles. Whatever the case, you need to identify the problem so you can compartmentalize it.

Step 2: Batch Your Work Into Playlists

My recommendation is to use playlists to batch your work, as I already briefly described.

What I like about iTunes' Playlists is you can create lists of tracks just by dragging songs into a Playlist without actually creating new copies of files. You can have one song in as many playlists as you want, while still maintaining just one copy of the file. Playlists are nothing more than classifications, and iTunes gives you great tools for viewing and managing them.

You can also create Smart Playlists, which are Playlists that iTunes generates automatically based on criteria you set, such as "songs I've skipped more than five times," or "songs I haven't played in more than one year." It's essentially an advanced search tool for creating Playlists.

How to create a Smart Playlist: Go to File > New > Smart Playlist. A new window will open in which you can enter the criteria you want.

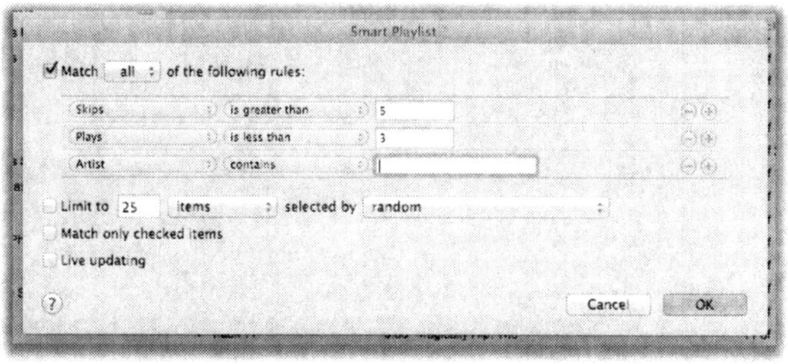

Figure 12-6: Smart Playlists in iTunes group together tracks based on what are essentially advanced search filters.

Use Playlists to cordon off the files that require your attention. Perhaps when you sorted by artist, you noticed a large number of files by "Madonna," which you're pretty sure are mislabeled (having the wrong metadata is common in music downloaded through peer-to-peer networks). Create a Playlist called "Not Madonna" or "Artists to Check" or something like that, and drag all the suspicious music into it.

How you name the Playlist is crucial. Think about what you learned when you surveyed your music, and try to come up with Playlist names that classify about 20 files. If you choose a name that encompasses too many files, you'll have an insurmountable cleanup task. If the name is too narrow, you'll be wasting a lot of time creating and naming Playlists when you could be doing something more productive. Twenty files, give or take a few, is not an overwhelming amount, and it's few enough to spot check as you go.

What you are really doing here on a conceptual level is batching your work. You're grouping together files that you will do more work on later. You're breaking down the huge project into smaller component parts.

Notice that you could stop and take a break at this point. It's easy to know exactly where you are in your cleanup effort. When you begin working with the batches, you'll have the same ability to do a little work and then stop when you need to, and pick it up again at a later date.

Tip:
Use a special character at the start
of your "batch" Playlist names.

I like to insert an underscore (_) at
the beginning so that all Playlists
that are essential work batches
float to the top of the left column,
where I can see them easily.

Step 3: Fix Your Music Files

Now, the "work" that you'll do with these batches largely depends
on your goal and the Playlist names you created. Are you adding
metadata? Are you checking that the songs have the correct labels?
Are you looking to delete duplicates that iTunes couldn't find?

Whatever the case, and no matter whether you're using tools
built into iTunes (such the iTunes Store to look up information)
or your own ad-hoc method (like holding up your smartphone
with the Shazam app running to figure out the name of a song),
spot-check your work as you go. Do a little at a time so that you
don't make mistakes or introduce incorrect metadata.

Step 4: Delete From Playlists

As you fix up files, delete them from the Playlist. Note that deleting from a Playlist is not the same as deleting the file. Deleting
songs from a Playlist does nothing more than remove the playlist
classification, which is essentially just a tag. If you're uncertain
whether you're deleting from the Playlist or about to delete the
file itself, don't worry: There is an "Are you sure?" pop-up that
more clearly states what you're about to do before you finalize the
action.

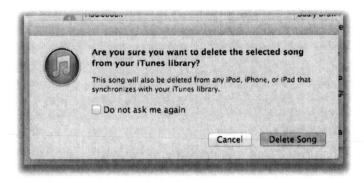

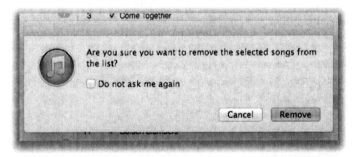

Figure 12-7: Be careful in iTunes to know when you are deleting a file (top image) and merely removing it from a Playlist (bottom image).

When a batch is done, delete the Playlist entirely.

Going through all your batches could take days or weeks or years, but that's okay. You're not meant to do it all at once. The batch method lets you break down a huge project into manageable pieces.

Working in small batches helps you keep an eye out for common problems (which you can read about in the Additional Content at the end of this chapter) that sometimes occur when cleaning up music files. These problems are harder to spot when you are trying to process, say, hundreds of files at once rather than merely dozens.

VI. HOW TO KEEP iTUNES BETTER ORGANIZED MOVING FORWARD

Now that you've done all this cleanup, I'm sure you'd rather automate it in the future. Here's how to enable the right settings so that the next time you import a CD, much of the work you've just done will happen automatically.

Go to iTunes > Preferences > General and look for the section "When you insert a CD." Tick the boxes for "Automatically retrieve CD track names from Internet" and "Automatically download missing album artwork." Most people will want both of those pieces of data, unless you're trying to minimize extraneous files, in which case perhaps ditch the album artwork. You now know how to get it later if you want it. If you're very visual, however, the album covers might be integral to your ability to use iTunes quickly and efficiently. It's your call.

VII. TAKE-AWAYS

- Cleaning up a music library shouldn't be about aiming for "perfection," but rather should be in line with some specific goal.
- Break down the task of cleaning up your music collection into smaller components that can be completed independently of one another.
- Take your time and work on reorganizing your music library a little here and a little there.
- Working in batches lets you spot-check to ensure you don't accidentally delete items you wanted to keep.

- To free up space on your computer, you can move music files to another place. You can also try excluding album artwork from your iTunes library.

VIII. RECOMMENDED SERVICES, SOFTWARE, AND HARDWARE

External hard drive (about $200). An external hard drive is a great place to move your music if it's taking up too much space locally. It's also useful for offloading music from your computer and saving it as a backup (and note that you should have an additional backup of these files, too). I personally like most of the models by LaCie, which tend to be very reliable and durable.

iCloud (free to $100 per year). You can turn on iCloud and delete all files you purchased through iTunes because you can always download them whenever you want them at no additional cost for up to 5GB. More space will cost you. Using iCloud is likely only a partial solution (unless you bought a significant portion of your music through iTunes), but depending on how much space you want to free up, this could be the simplest and least expensive option.

iTunes Match ($24.99 per year for up to 25,000 songs). Simple, fairly inexpensive, and reasonably straightforward, iTunes Match will scan your music library and, if it finds songs in its database that you have in iTunes, it will essentially give you a license to download or stream that song any time you want. If it doesn't have matches, you can upload your music, and the same deal applies. If you're typically connected to the Internet when you listen to music, the streaming capability makes iTunes Match a pretty good deal.

TuneUp ($49.95). If you want to use an outside tool that will identify misnamed tracks or songs that are missing information, TuneUp is a good bet. It fills in missing metadata, including song lyrics if you like, and includes some extra features such as concert notifications of music acts you like.

- Additional Content -

How to Check How Much Space Your Music Collection Uses

At the bottom of the iTunes window is a bar showing how much
total space your music collection uses.

In the above image, you can see that the size of my music collection is 5.16GB and that I have 1,091 total items. Sure, it's not a
huge number, but some of my individual tracks are quite large:
audio books, 30-minute language-learning audio files, etc.

   That number is what you need to determine how much space
your collection will take up if you move it to another location. It
differs from what you'll see if you right-click on the iTunes folder
in the default location and pull up information about how much
total space that folder is using.

In the above image, you can see that the total size for the folder is 8.59GB. The reason for the difference? It contains additional data, including organizational information, such as data used to create Smart Playlists. Those files should remain in the original location. Don't move or delete them!

Finally, how big is the iTunes program itself? According to Apple, iTunes 11.0.4 is 187.52MB for the OS X version, 84.98MB for the 32-bit Windows version, and 86.71MB for the 64-bit Windows version.

-

- Additional Content -

Typical iTunes Trip-ups

When you try to clean up iTunes using some of the built-in tools (as well as third-party cleaning apps), there are a couple of common problems that may occur. Keep an eye out for these by working in small batches, as I suggested earlier.

"Featuring" artist listed as artist. When one musical artist appears as a guest on someone else's album, that guest is sometimes listed as "featuring." iTunes can sometimes mistakenly identify the song as being by the featured artist, thereby incorrectly grouping it when you sort by artist or album. When updating fields, make sure that the artist is the one you want, which in most cases is whichever artist is listed on the album—not the song.

Compilations. I mentioned previously that if you only have one piece of information about a music file, the correct album name is the most valuable, something that is especially important with compilation albums. When checking over compilation albums, make sure the album name stays intact.

Songs on multiple albums. Another problem that can happen when you have compilation albums in the mix is that one song appears on more than one album. Sometimes it's the same recording, in which case you can delete the duplicate. But sometimes it's a new recording and you want to keep both versions. For example, the song "We've Only Just Begun" by The Carpenters is the first track of two albums: Close to You and The Singles: 1969-1973. Pay attention to the song length. If they don't match exactly, the songs are probably different.

13

Social Media

Plenty of people use a number of different social networking sites, and I am one of them. Whether the purpose is to stay connected to friends and family, to get updates about what's happening in the world, or to find suitable job candidates, your social media use can easily get out of hand and become disorganized.

This chapter names a few social media sites that I think most people would benefit for using. I'll also walk you through a few simple practices that will help you keep your overall social online presence clean, neat, and organized.

What won't be covered in this chapter is what to do with *photos* you might collect on social media. For that, see Chapter 11.

I. FACEBOOK

The majority of people I know have at least one Facebook account, and a few people have more than one. (If you don't have a Facebook account, I am by no means advocating you start one, but I'd hedge my bets that most people reading this book do in fact have one already.)

Facebook is one of those highly active social networking sites where the amount of data on it can become overwhelming, especially when you aren't the person posting it all. Tagged photos, inappropriate comments, and connected services that post status updates on your behalf are only the tip of the iceberg in terms of problems.

Facebook Activity Log

If your Facebook account predates your, ahem, current maturity level (for example, if you worry some old and forgotten Facebook photos of you doing keg stands will come back to haunt you), you can hand-pick through your content easiest using the Activity Log, which you can find on your profile page.

Figure 13-1. Facebook's Activity log lets you manually review and clean up posts, tagged photos, and more.

The Activity Log lets you drill down by content type, such as photos, photos of you, tagged photos, and so forth, so you can focus on one area of your Facebook account at a time while finding images to delete or hide.

Simplewa.sh

There's also a free tool that can help you root out all that nonsense called Simplewa.sh. Simplewa.sh is a simple, if slightly imperfect, free tool that helps you find inappropriate content on your Facebook account (it also works on Twitter). It scours your account and compares all the text it finds, including photo captions and comments from other people on your Facebook account, against a list of bad words. The list goes well beyond the dirty words not allowed on network television and includes things like "beer" and "sexy." Once Simplewa.sh finds the content, it helps you edit or remove it by directing you to the page or post where it lives—you still have to manually hide or delete it. You can also use Simplewa.sh to search for specific words, which is handy in a number of different scenarios, such as before going on a job interview if you want to check whether you've posted anything publically about the company in question.

Annual checklist: Once a year (or more), review your Facebook app permissions and remove anything that you aren't actively using anymore. Also review and update your privacy settings and contact information.

II. TWITTER

Although Twitter might not be for everyone, I do think it is an invaluable network for people in a number of fields, including education, technology, journalism, communications, government or public office, entertainment, activism, and so many others.

Unless you keep your Twitter account private (meaning the only people who can see your tweets are those you've given permission to follow you), I advocate erring on the side of professionalism with Twitter. Perhaps that advice is grounded in my own experience on the site (I'm @jilleduffy, if you care to follow me...), but I tend to uncover some very interesting professional opportunities via the site. What I mean by that is people find me through

Twitter and ask me to speak at events, meet with influential people to share ideas, work on new projects, and so forth.

Your Bio and the Topic of Your Tweets

If you're using Twitter to promote yourself or your job (meaning you actively want to gain more followers), your bio is one of the most important areas of Twitter to keep well organized, clean, and thoughtfully presented.

Your Twitter bio is a promise to potential new followers and the community in general that you're on Twitter to share information and ideas about whatever it is you mention in your bio. Your bio, therefore, should match the content of your tweets, at least 70 percent of the time. If you use Twitter to talk about food and recipes, your bio should reflect that. If you use Twitter to talk to other educators about matters related to public schools in Iowa, you need to present that fact in your bio.

If you only use Twitter lightly and aren't interested in gaining more followers, then this concept of matching the content of your tweets to your Twitter bio isn't so important. But if you are pushing a message or trying to increase your presence online, it's extremely important.

What's with the "70 percent of the time" clause, then? Well, Twitter is a social network, and most people will agree that it's perfectly fine to be off-topic some of the time to let your personality shine through. Just try not to do it too much.

III. BUSINESS: LINKEDIN

I'm of the mind that every adult-aged person should have a LinkedIn profile. It's perhaps the biggest professional online network that crosses industries and penetrates dozens of countries the world over.

One of the "organizational" reasons I like LinkedIn is that it acts like a secondary contacts database. You might keep all the contact information for your closest friends, family, and business associates in your address book, and maybe you have another contact database in your email program, but LinkedIn lets you go well beyond them and in a way that takes some of the organizing pressure off you. Why? LinkedIn works in large part on the premise that every user updates his or her own information. That means you are not responsible for updating someone's email address after they change jobs and have a new account at a new company. It's that person's responsibility to update the information in LinkedIn.

LinkedIn is as much about staying connected to others as it is about putting yourself out there. You can see updates regarding how many people looked at your profile, and some of the names of people who checked out your profile (the information is somewhat limited unless you pay for an account).

Fill out your LinkedIn profile carefully and with the same mindfulness that you would use to create a resume. Use the same brevity that you might exercise on a resume as well—you don't need to list on LinkedIn every achievements and skills. Just cover the most important aspects of your professional life that you want other people to know about.

Figure 13-2. LinkedIn has a terrific feature that shows you how many people have peered at your profile recently. Premium account holders can see even more details regarding exactly who looked at their profile.

Annual checklist: It's a good idea to review your LinkedIn profile once a year to make sure it's up to date so that other people can find you.

II. ADDITIONAL TIPS AND TOOLS FOR KEEPING UP YOUR SOCIAL SITES

When you think about organizing your social media sites, you should consider not just each individual site, but also your overall strategy and presence. These tips relate to your social media accounts as well as any blogs or websites that you run. If you don't have your own website or blog, you can still recreate the experience of having a unique page that's just about you (and not about, say, Facebook) by setting up a custom landing page—see the Additional Content at the end of this chapter for more details.

Brand Your Identity

All the online handles or usernames you choose either act to strengthen or weaken your overall online presence. For example, if you secured the Gmail address MadelineRCrumb, you might use that same moniker for Twitter, and the same ending for your Facebook.com URL (Facebook.com/MadelineRCrumb), and so on.

If you stick with one handle for all your sites and services, you will project a more cohesive identity. On the other hand, you might purposefully use different handles to differentiate, say, your personal Twitter account from your professional Flavors.me page.

Profile Photo

Similar to how a consistent handle or username across sites helps to project a single, clean identity, having the same profile pictures on all your social networks does the same thing.

Take multiple photos, maybe even up to 50 of them, until you have one that is flattering while still looking like you. It should show your face, a bit of neck, and some of your shoulders, which you can crop out later, depending on the image size you need. (People used to refer to this style of photo as a "head and shoulders shot," which is where we get the shortened "headshot.") Smile, use props or backdrops to portray something about your work or personality if you like, and most important of all, pick a photo that you will be happy with for at least a year so that you don't change it too often. For more tips on choosing the right profile picture, see the Additional Content at the end of this chapter.

Profile photo dimensions tend to be square, so keep that in mind when you crop the image. And editing the photo to minimize blemishes, eliminate red-eye, and otherwise make the image look more appealing is totally fine—nay, outright encouraged.

Annual checklist: If you're aiming for professionalism, I recommend updating your photo no more than once a year.

ifttt

ifttt (short for "if this, then that") is a free site and service you use to create little commands across the Internet, such as "if someone tags me on Facebook, then send me a text message alert." It actually has applications that go well beyond helping you manage and organize your social media accounts, but there are a few neat commands, called "recipes," you can set up that very specifically take care of your presence on Twitter, Facebook, LinkedIn, Google+, YouTube, Instagram, and many other social media accounts.

For example, you can set up an automation such that when you update your Twitter profile picture, your Facebook profile picture also updates to the same one. You can also write a recipe so that all the links you share on Facebook are also saved to a Google Drive spreadsheet (very useful if you need to keep track of what you share for business purposes). Another nice recipe: "If I post something on Twitter (or Facebook for that matter), then also post it to Google+"—a great workaround for the problem of not being able to directly connect your Google+ account to Twitter and Facebook.

Figure 13-3. You can use ifttt to quickly create commands to help you stay organized across your social media accounts. No programming knowledge is needed to use the site.

ifttt leaves a lot of room for creativity, because it connects to dozens of social networks, Internet services, and other technology.

TweetDeck, HootSuite

TweetDeck and HootSuite are two social media aggregators that I like. They compile updates and activity from multiple social networks so that you can see content from your Twitter stream and Facebook feed in one place. TweetDeck is also helpful if you need to manage your own postings to multiple social networks because it lets you schedule posts to appear at a certain time, so you can write them all in the morning, but schedule them to post once an hour, or throughout the night, or what have you.

Cloze

Cloze is a neat service that's sort of an aggregator, but does it a little differently than TweetDeck and HootSuite—and it connects to email accounts. Instead of simply compiling the activity into one place, Cloze also ranks it based on your relationship to the person who posted it. If Cloze determines that your boss, sister, and mother-in-law are all important people, based on how often you email them or how quickly you reply to posts they create, it will show you tweets and posts from them first, and activity from the rest of your community later.

Figure 13-4. Cloze is a tool that shows you social media updates, emails, and other bits of communication only from people who are most important to you.

Cloze is great for making sure you don't miss social networking information and emails from people who are (or should be) important.

III. TAKE-AWAYS

- Use social media to connect with friends, network professionally, and make yourself available to find for new professional (and personal) opportunities.

- Online social networks, particularly LinkedIn, can help you keep contact information about your professional network up to date no matter where you currently work or live.
- On LinkedIn, less is often more. You don't need to list every single skill and job you've ever had—just the ones you want people to know about.
- Having your own website or blog is a good way to make yourself known online, although you can also set up a free landing page to the same end.
- Use the same profile photo and handle across social networks for a more consistent and branded identity.
- Update your profile photo no more than once a year if you're aiming for consistency, visibility, and self-branding.
- Keep your Facebook and Twitter accounts "clean" by using tools like Simplewa.sh to root out inappropriate content.
- Use social media aggregation tools to help you stay on top of the never-ending flood of content, or to post to social networks more often with greater ease.

IV. RECOMMENDED TOOLS

- About.me
- Cloze
- Facebook
- Flavors.me
- Google+
- HootSuite

- LinkedIn
- Pinterest
- Simplewa.sh
- TweetDeck
- Twitter
- Vimeo
- YouTube

- Additional Content -

Tips for Getting a Great Profile Picture

When it comes time to shoot a new profile photo or choose one from among some existing shots, you may want to rely on a friend's judgment. It's tough for a lot of people to choose a photograph that genuinely looks like them in real life. We can get wrapped up trying to find the perfect image that we think looks the most flattering, whereas our friends are usually better at making an objective call about which image actually looks like us and still looks good.

A friend can also come in handy if you have to take a new photo. If you prefer a solo photo shoot, use the timer on your camera and set it on a tripod or a flat and steady surface—for example, a stack of books on a table. Do not hold the camera at arm's length and take a selfie. Just don't.

Take a lot of photos—at least 30 or 40—before you pick one. It might take more than 50 before you get one shot you like. Be patient, and bear in mind that it will be worth it in the long run.

You'll be getting a lot of use out of one image. And smile. Smile with teeth. Smile without teeth. Don't be afraid to try a few different poses. Sometimes you can't tell what works and what doesn't until you review a bunch of photos after the fact.

You'll also want a photo that genuinely reflects who you are and shows your best qualities. Your facial expression will do most of the talking here, but you can also use props, wardrobe choices, and scenery to your advantage. For example, if you wear glasses, leave them on for the photo. If you're known by your colleagues as "the guy who lives in Alaska," shoot outdoors with the landscape visible. If you're known for having a very business-like demeanor and that's how you want others to see you, take a straight headshot with a solid colored background.

Seeing as most people won't have access to a photo studio, use natural sunlight to your advantage. Shoot outdoors or in a room that's bright with sunlight. Remember to pay attention to what's in the background, but also know that you can crop or retouch the image later if it's not picture-perfect.

-

- Additional Content -

What If You Don't Have Your Own Blog or Website?

A custom URL, such as a personal website or blog, helps others find you online. So what should you do if you don't have your own site and frankly aren't interested in starting one?

A simple alternative is to create a free "landing page." Think of it like having an online business card, a splashy picture or logo with a few lines describing who you are and what you do, plus any contact information you want to include on it. It's much easier to set up and maintain than a complete website or blog that you would feel obligated to update frequently. (See an example at http://flavors.me/jilleduffy.)

A few services that let you create a custom landing page are Jux.com, About.me and Flavors.me. Typically, they offer you an array of templates that suggest a minimal amount of text paired with one or two large graphics.

Both a custom website and a free landing page are useful links to provide in your other social media bios and in an email signature line so that you can direct people to a place where they can learn more about what you do and what you offer.

-

14

Personal Finance

Money, or the lack of it, causes a lot of undue stress. Few people have a firm grip on their personal financial situation, and those who do rarely arrived at economic stability by chance. Even those born into wealth don't necessarily have a clear picture of their money, how they spend it, when new income is available, and so forth.

To have a good understanding of your own money and assets takes a keen awareness of one's lifestyle, some planning, an ounce of discipline, and a little organization. But anyone can get there with the right tools and the right attitude.

A few years ago, one of my friends, who is from a well-to-do family and has never wanted for money in his life, confessed to me that he had no idea how much he spent every month. He had never drawn up a budget. He didn't know his net worth. I don't think he even knew he had interest income. Now, as an adult, the stark realization that he really ought to know something about his money loomed over him, creating anxiety, guilt, and self-doubt.

He came to me for advice. He said he needed to learn something about managing money and budgeting to feel like a capable adult.

I did not grow up in a household that managed its finances well, but I learned a lot from my parents' mistakes. As an adult, I have managed to stay out of debt, pay off my student loans early, contribute to a couple of retirement accounts, and diversify my investments. I'm no millionaire, but I have a plan that I follow, and I feel secure financially, which is probably the most important financial goal I have.

My friend and I talked through some basic strategies, some of which I'll share in this chapter, and he was able to see his finances clearly in about three months.

My friend's story is rare. The majority of people I know who struggle with their finances are crippled by debt, not flush with cash, but it just goes to show that the problem is not necessarily how much money you have, but whether you know where it comes from and where it needs to go.

I think a big fear for many people who don't know the first thing about their personal finances is math. Numbers intimidate a lot of people. The good news is that software programs, online tools, and basic information available online can do all the calculations for you. Your job is simply to use the right tools for your situation and stick to the rules you put in place for yourself and your money.

I. PERSONAL FINANCE FOR BEGINNERS

If you're brand new to understanding your finances, the very first thing you need to do is figure out how you currently spend your monthly income, and the way to do that is to write down everything you buy or pay, including bills and subscriptions. Don't worry about income just yet.

You can write down what you spend manually in a note-taking app or spreadsheet, or by using personal finance software. Writing down what you spend manually may sound tedious and pointless, considering you could use an app to do it for you, but it's a great way to become more intimate with every dollar you earn and spend. I'll cover the manual way first and the automatic way second.

How to Manually Log Expenses

One method of logging is to create a simple note on your mobile phone and log on it everything you buy on the go. Jot down the date, total spent, what you purchased, and what form of payment you used so that it's easy to reconcile your credit card bills. You can then transfer your notes into a spreadsheet at the end of the day. Also include on this spreadsheet other expenses, like your rent or mortgage payment, bills, subscriptions—everything.

	A	B	C	D	E
Total		**Budget Category**	**Details**	**Seller**	**Date**
	-$13.00	groceries	coffee beans	Blue Bottle	8/1/2013
	-$208.95	clothing	work clothes	Modcloth (online)	8/1/2013
	-$200.00	gift	wedding gift	Mary and Fabian	8/1/2013
	$3.29	interest	savings account interest	Bank	8/1/2013
	-$2.75	household	laundry	laundry machines	8/3/2013
	-$27.95	transportation	bicycle gloves	Paragon Sports	8/3/2013
	-$8.79	restaurants	lunch out	Sushi Bar	8/5/2013

Figure 14-1. Keeping track of how much you spend, whether it's in a personal finance app or just on a simple spreadsheet, as shown here, is the first step to understanding your finances.

Alternatively, you could use a receipt-scanning smartphone app such as ReceiptsPro ($4.99) or NeatMobile (from $5.99 per month, with a NeatCloud account), but these apps will run you a few bucks and who knows yet if you can afford them (I'm kidding—sort of).

If keeping a note on your phone and a spreadsheet on your computer doesn't sound advanced enough, you could buy YNAB ($60), a budgeting software program. (Its name stands for You Need a Budget.) It's a desktop application that's extremely well suited for beginners because it includes a lot of information about a couple of rules behind the budgeting philosophy it uses to help you manage your money. YNAB will have you log your expenses manually, at least at first while you're getting set up, so you'll still get that benefit of having to think about every dollar you spend.

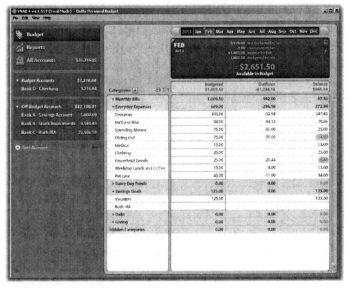

Figure 14-2. YNAB is a good piece of personal finance software for beginners in particular because it includes a lot of helpful advice and education about managing money.

Don't forget to also log automatic credit card or debit account transactions, such as gym membership fees, automated donations, and automatic bill payments.

How to Log Expenses Automatically

My favorite tool for automatically watching what you spend is Mint.com (free). Mint and its mobile apps work by linking directly into all your financial accounts, from checking and savings accounts to credit cards and loans. It looks at your credit card and debit accounts, and classifies all your spending into categories, such as clothes, food, gas, entertainment, and much more.

Mint shows you your real-time net worth or total debt, depending on whether you're in the red or black, which changes from day to day. Mint has a lot more to offer than just that, but for now all you need to know is that Mint will automatically track all your spending and show you all kinds of charts and information about your expenses.

Regardless of how your track your spending, it will take several weeks of logging before you can see how much you spend on average per week or per month. No month is ever as "normal" as you think it will be. There are always unexpected expenses, such as car repairs, gifts, emergency travel, unexpected health care costs, and on and on. Do include these unexpected expenses as you track your spending! Categorize them as "unexpected" or "emergency" to see how these unanticipated costs average out over time. After you've recorded expenses for a few weeks (I'd recommend a minimum of three months), you can start to average them to get a better understanding of your expenditures.

II. BASIC BUDGETING

Only after you start to have a clear understanding of where you're actually spending your money can you think about truly budgeting it. To budget, you'll need to know how much money you earn, too. If you have a fairly simple income that consists of nothing more than a paycheck, this step will be very straightforward. But if you have any additional income, whether from earned interest or additional work, you'll want to include that as well. If your income fluctuates each month, track it just the way you would your expenses to determine the average.

Perhaps in the course of writing down what you spend day to day, you've already identified places where you can cut back.

Good. That's the whole point of creating an awareness of your spending.

Now's the time to deploy a more rigorous personal finance and budgeting application. The steps look something like this:

- track all your expenses
- classify all your spending
- figure out your monthly income or average monthly income
- create new categories of spending for your personal finance goals (such as saving to buy a house or for retirement)
- based on your findings of categorized spending, create budgets to keep your spending in line such that the total amount spent is less than average monthly income
- use a smartphone app to help keep your spending within the set budgets.

So far I've covered the first three points. The next one is to set some financial goals. A few examples of financial goals are saving up for a family vacation, getting out of debt, buying a home, and hitting a specified figure in your retirement funds. These goals should become their own expenditure lines in your budget. Classify them appropriately, and treat them as necessary but flexible expenses but flexible, just as you would many of your other categories. Flexible expenses are budgeting categories that you have some control over, such your budget for entertainment and food. Fixed expenses, on the other hand, are those that you have no control over, such as your rent or mortgage payment.

The point of a budgeting application is to help you set different limits on your own spending in different categories. Because you'll already know the basic breakdown of your spending, it should be fairly simple to adjust your various money allotments in categories that are flexible. For example, maybe you didn't before realize you spend an average of $75 a month on average on music and movie downloads. If that amount seems high to you, you can think about restricting the total to, say $20 per month and using the remaining $55 to pay down debts or put into savings.

As you continue to budget your money and watch your income and expenses change over time, allow yourself the ability to correct course as needed. You probably won't find a sweet spot for saving and spending right away, and that's okay. Budgets should be somewhat adjustable to accommodate your circumstances.

If you use YNAB, definitely look into all tutorials and advice that come included with the software. They can walk you through a lot of basic budgeting principles. I'll have a few more recommended places for learning more about budgeting in the next section.

With Mint, you can set up personalized budgets for various categories of expenses, as well as goals, such as saving for a vacation. Because Mint automatically categorizes money you spend (per transaction), it can alert you when you're about to go over budget in any given category.

Figure 14-3. Mint is one of the best-known personal finance solutions. It is cloud-based and accessible through a Web browser as well as a mobile app.

Even though Mint is a pretty exceptional tool, it isn't all hunky-dory. When you spend cash, you have to manually enter the category of everything you bought. And you'll likely have to make a few tweaks to some of the automations that can be annoying at first, although Mint learns from the corrections you make over time. For example, when I first used Mint, I spent more time than seemed worthwhile coding a few recurring payments. Mint kept thinking a payment to "Duffy" meant "Dr. Duffy," which was thus classified as a medical expense when in reality, it was a straight transfer of funds from one of my accounts to another. When mistakes like this one occur, you can reclassify the transaction and tell Mint to always classify it the way you've marked it.

Setting your budgets for different categories is one thing. Sticking to them is harder and takes some self-discipline. Having a smartphone app with some budgeting information on it helps because it can be in front of your eyes at all times, including when you're about to make an impulse purchase.

Managing your own money is one thing, but taking charge of household expenses is another matter. The principles are the same—get a grip on all the expenditures, analyze whether you're spending too much in any given area, set a budget for future spending in that area—but the capacity is different. You have to think about and try to curb not only your own spending habits, but also those of other people in your home.

The online Doxo.com lets you manage household payments, connect with utility and service providers, and backup important family documents while you're at it (think last year's taxes), so it does double duty. Think of it like an online filing cabinet. It's not for budgeting exactly, but it does have some useful tools that relate to budgeting. For example, Doxo lets you view all your e-statements at once across a whole bunch of different service providers and billers. It also connects to healthcare providers so that you can see medical statements, all in the same place as your other bills. It's well worth signing up for Doxo if your real filing cabinet is in shambles.

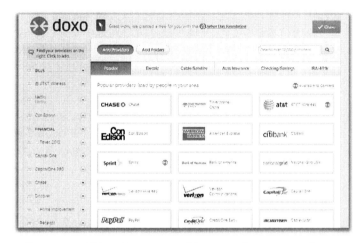

Figure 14-4. Although not personal finance software per se, Doxo is another service that helps you organize and manage household accounts and bills. It also consolidates e-statements from numerous providers into one place and lets you upload important documents to save to your account, too.

III. PERSONAL FINANCE EDUCATION AND ONLINE CALCULATORS

Once you get a handle on your income and spending, and start living by your budget, you might want to start thinking about other ways you can make your money work for you. One of the biggest financial decisions people make is whether to buy or rent a home. I'm a huge fan of the education website Khan Academy, which just happens to have a stellar nine-minute video that explains some of the difference in cost between renting and buying. Watch it for an overview, then do a little more research about the area in which you live. Home values are location dependent, so the numbers you'll need to decide whether to rent or buy (annual expected increase in rent, expected appreciation of the value of the home, etc.) could vary dramatically between, say, Toronto and Tuskegee, Alabama.

I'll confess to having used the *New York Times'* rent-versus-buy calculator because the newspaper builds into its system different payments associated with owning a co-op apartment or condos, which are common in my city.

Another common investment that people want to better manage is their retirement account. Rather than throw in "as much as I feel comfortable contributing each month," use the calculators provided by your retirement account provider. They all have them. Spend a few minutes deciding how much money you would like to have available when you retire (remembering to account for inflation, which the calculator should do for you automatically), and what the monthly payout would be if you live to a ripe old age. In other words, work backward. And of course, find out if your employer matches a percent of your contribution. If you're not taking advantage by contributing the full amount that the organization will match, you are essentially lowering your own total compensation.

Watch:

"Online Retirement Account Calculator,"
part of the Get Organized Video Series,
at bit.ly/RetireCalculator

Like any lifestyle change, getting a grip on your personal finances and putting yourself on a budget takes constant vigilance, at least at first while you're trying to build an awareness of your money and spending habits. For this reason, smartphone apps can really help you stick to your goals, such as writing down your purchases or keeping an eye on your checking account balance, because they're always with you. Use these tools, and professional financial advice if needed, to create a plan for your money and remove some of that unnecessary stress that comes with having disorganized finances.

BUSINESS:: Read the Additional Content at the end of this chapter for advice on simple financial software for small business and freelancers.

IV. TAKE-AWAYS

- Track how much money you spend before doing any other personal finance and budgeting work
- Use a spreadsheet or an automated tool to account for your expenses and classify them
- Based on your findings of categorized spending, create budgets to keep your spending in line.
- Include in your budget personal finance goals, such as getting out of debt or saving up to buy a home.
- Use a smartphone app to help keep your spending within the set budgets.
- Adjust your budget over time to correct course and accommodate changes in your lifestyle.

V. RECOMMENDED TOOLS

- FreshBooks (business)
- Khan Academy
- Mint.com
- NeatMobile
- New York Times rent-versus-buy calculator
- OfficeTime (business)
- Outright (business)
- Quicken
- ReceiptsPro
- YNAB
- Zoho Invoice (business)

- Additional Content -

Simple Finance Software for Small Businesses & Freelancers

Small business owners, freelancers, and other independent workers have a much bigger job on their hands than even the most complicated household when it comes to managing money. When small businesses first get off the ground, an accounting and invoicing system isn't always necessary. You find work. You complete the work. You get paid. Simple enough. But gradually, sometimes imperceptibly so, the situation changes. Get yourself or your micro business organized by picking the right kind of system and putting it in place now—even if you wish you had done it long ago. It will make it easier to grow your business later.

Solo freelancers and other self-employed people in a one-man shop likely don't need a highly advanced financial application for managing accounts and invoicing. What's more, you shouldn't pay an arm and a leg for a long list of features you simply won't use. Stick with a simple program that gets the job done and doesn't cost much, such as FreshBooks, which has client and product/service records, easy invoice creation and dispatching, and solid features for running reports. Quicken is another popular accounting software option for small businesses.

A more simplified tool that's good for anyone who charges by the hour is OfficeTime, which tracks how much time you spend on projects while you're working and creates invoices based on that data. The invoicing component is enough for most solo operations.

Other good free options include Zoho Invoice, which doesn't have time tracking or timesheets, and Outright, which is specifically designed for very small businesses that don't handle inventory or payroll.

15

Preparing for Digital Afterlife

Although it's not a pleasant topic of conversation, figuring out what will happen to your digital life after you die is something that every organized and responsible person should do.

A last will and testament and other standard forms can help you make arrangements for what will happen to your money, property, physical assets, and dependents (such as children) after you die. But they typically don't take into consideration your digital life, which could have a lot of value, whether financial or sentimental. More importantly, the information contained in a deceased person's email accounts, social media accounts, and other virtual places could also have much-needed information relating to the cause of death.

If you've ever been the executor of a will, you know it can take months just to get through the paperwork and distribution of assets as outlined in a last will and testament—and those are routine legal procedures. So just imagine what you might have to endure to recover a loved one's domain name, email address, Facebook page, and so on.

Implementing a strategy for how you can pass on your digital assets after you die is actually a lot less complicated than you might assume.

A few caveats, however, are:

- You typically give only access to only one person, so you can't have multiple beneficiaries for your digital accounts.
- With most of the solutions, you have to trust that the beneficiary won't log in on your behalf before your demise. Sometimes there is a contingency in place that prevents the person from getting access to your accounts until after you die, in which case...
- There could be a time lag if the beneficiary has to provide a death certificate.
- Regardless, the benefits of having a system to pass on access to your digital assets trump all the minor nuisances and stipulations.

Here are the basic steps you need to take, some options for products you can use, and other tips for carrying out different strategies.

I. PICK A STRATEGY

There are a few different options for how you can pass on your digital assets, and you're not limited to using just one.

Option 1: Give Someone You Trust Your Primary Email Login

One of the simplest and most straightforward ways of passing on your assets is to give a partner, spouse, caretaker, or some other trusted individual your username and password combinations for your primary email account. Your trusted executor can perform password retrievals on any site on which he or she knows you have an account. I know a lot of couples who share their login information with one another, so as long as you make sure your partner has your primary email login, you'll be set.

If you use Gmail, Google has a feature called Inactive Account manager, which lets you set up a timer and notification, such that if you don't log in to Google for the amount of time you set, Google will notify whomever you list as a trusted contact in this setting, up to ten people. (It's actually hard to find this setting in a Google account, so just do a search for "Google Inactive Account manager.")

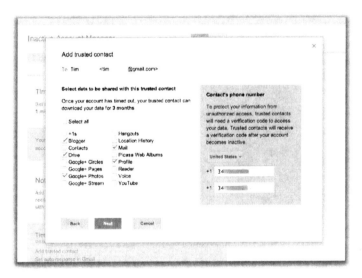

Figure 15-1. Google's Inactive Account manager lets you pass on your Google services to another person or multiple people in the event you die or become incapacitated. You can choose who gets access to what.

You can choose which Google services the person can access: Gmail, Google+, photos, YouTube, Google Voice, etc. In the last step, you can customize a message that Google will send to your trusted people so they are clear about what's happening.

Figure 15-2. When you set up the Google Inactive Account manager, you have the ability to customize a message that your designee will receive after you have not logged in to Google for a predetermined amount of time (at which time you are presumed incapacitated).

If you use the inactive account manager tool, there will be a known delay between the time you stop logging into Google and the time your beneficiary gets access. The shortest amount of time Google lets you choose is three months, a good idea, really—a power outage, minor injuries, or any number of other circumstances could prevent you from logging in to Google for a few weeks at a time. You wouldn't want have to recite that old Monty Python joke, "I'm not dead yet!"

However you pass on access to your primary email address, you need to check that all your important accounts are tied to it so that the person can recover passwords from other sites, or at the very least that this email address can be used to recover passwords for other email accounts you have.

To be perfectly honest, I personally would not give my designee access to my primary email account and expect the person to take over all my digital accounts that way. The main problem is that person won't have a list of all my account logins. If the person is close to you, he or she will likely know and remember that you have certain social media accounts enabled and whatnot, but there could be other accounts that simply slip his or her mind, especially when under duress.

Another problem is that for certain accounts, your trusted person may be asked to answer additional security questions. Does your partner know the make and model of your first car, your father's city of birth? How will you be sure your beneficiary knows or can figure out that information as well?

Although this first solution isn't ideal, it is extremely simple to implement, so if you're a procrastinator and know yourself well enough to admit that you're not going to follow through on a more thorough plan, it might be a good option for you. But one more thing to bear in mind: This solution puts accountability on the other person for remembering your login, which could be either good or bad, depending on how organized he or she is!

Option 2: Give Up Your Password Manager

Similar to the email account idea, you could give one trusted person the login information to your password manager, seeing as you've read Chapter 5 and now have a password manager. Some password managers actually have a feature or policy in their terms of service regarding passing on the information to a trusted individual after you die. I'll review those in the final section of this chapter on recommended tools.

Tip:

A quick refresher on password managers:
Password managers securely store all your
logins and passwords behind one login.
That means you only have to remember
one username and password code to
unlock everything else. Many password
managers are free, so your beneficiary
can simply download the app and log in
as you to unlock everything else you have
stored in there. For more, see Chapter 5.

One password manager called PasswordBox includes a setting
for naming a beneficiary of your passwords (there are more details
in the recommended tools and services section).

Figure 15-3. PasswordBox is one password manager with a feature for passing on access to the service after you die.

Option 3: Use a Specialty Digital Afterlife Service

The most thorough way to pass on your passwords and account information after you die is to use a service or software that specializes in just this very thing. They typically cost a little bit of money, ranging from a monthly charge to a one-time or "lifetime" (quite literally) fee. They take a little bit of time to set up. But as I said, they are thorough.

One option outlined in the recommended list later in this chapter, called Javont Vault, is desktop software rather than an online or cloud-based solution, so it's very secure because only someone with access to your computer, or the backup drive that comes included with the program, could possibly get her hands on your information. The other cool feature of Javont Vault is how many categories it has for listing all your assets—both digital and otherwise, as Javont Vault doesn't restrict you to just the virtual world. The hitch? The beneficiary needs your Social Security number to unlock the "vault" of information.

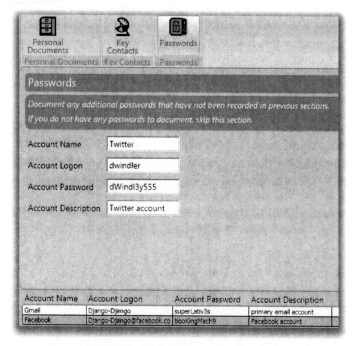

Figure 15-4. Javont Vault is specialty software for passing on access to your digital life after you die. It is specifically designed for this use, and therefore is quite thorough.

II. Inform the Recipient

Once you've picked a solution for passing on your passwords, you need to make sure your beneficiary is aware of his or her role. I recommend having a face-to-face or telephone conversation first wherein you ask your intended beneficiary if she or he is okay with these duties. Not everyone wants to take on such a grim role. You should then send an email with a very clear subject line, such as "emergency information for Jill Duffy's digital accounts." CC yourself on the email, or save a copy in your sent mail.

The body of the email should outline the instructions for how you want the beneficiary to carry out the role. For example, if you're in a coma, do you want someone to post a status update about your condition to your Facebook page? Should this person send an email on your behalf? If you die, are there any drafts of emails to loved ones for which you want the person to hit "send?" Should your beneficiary delete your social media accounts, and if so, immediately or after a set amount of time?

Your email with instructions could be more vague. It might say, "Depending on the circumstances of my condition, I trust you to make decisions regarding my online accounts." Or it could be somewhere in between: "Please talk to Cindy about Accounts X and Y, as she will likely know how best to handle them."

III. MAKE SURE THE STRATEGY IS CURRENT

Last wills and testaments can sometimes be out of date by the time a person passes away, although they're also often structured so they reflect the passage of time. Legalese will say, "Do X, unless Y occurs, in which case, do Z." And the paperwork itself is overseen by a professional who knows to keep a vigilant eye on such issues.

When you're passing on your own digital information without legal counsel, you should check that the information is current at least once a year.

Annual checklist: Review the email you saved that outlines the instructions for your beneficiary. Are the instructions still accurate? Have any of your logins changed? Have you added any new important accounts? Is the beneficiary still using the same email address (if not, she or he may have abandoned this important email from you in the old account)? Do you want your beneficiary to be someone else now?

Update anything that needs updating, and resend the message. Again, CC yourself or save the sent mail so that you can refer to the message next year, too.

IV. RECOMMENDED TOOLS AND SERVICES

Dashlane (Password Manager)

Dashlane, as of this writing, does not have any special features or services for helping you transfer the account to another person if you die or become incapacitated. But it's a good password manager anyway, and there are plenty of ways you can give the username and password of your Dashlane account to a beneficiary.

Google Inactive Account

If you use Gmail or other Google services, I highly recommend enabling the inactive account feature. Be sure to take your time writing that custom email that the beneficiary will receive so she or he knows what to do. I would recommend granting someone access to your email and photos first, and any other parts of Google you use that you want someone to manage or archive on your behalf.

Javont Vault

Unlike most "digital afterlife" products, Javont Vault is Windows desktop software that takes a comprehensive approach to documenting your assets, both real-world and virtual. The fact that it resides locally on your computer and doesn't connect to the Internet at all adds a layer of security, too. This program lets you catalog everything—possessions, safety deposit box information, passwords, and even memberships—in one place where your next of kin can get it fairly easily after you're gone, so long as they can get onto your computer and know your social security number.

The software categorizes all your assets by type (banking, investment, insurance, household bills, and so forth), making it extremely easy to fill in various sections according to what you own. A section called File Cabinet has a subsection for Passwords where you enter information about all your online accounts. The other sections and subsections, like the Credit Cards subsection of Banking, also have fields for entering the online login information you use to access those accounts. Javont Vault even includes a category for utility bills that you might manage online.

Javont's design takes into consideration how your next of kin will unlock your virtual vault to access the information they'll need. The only real sticking point for potential Javont Vault users is that the product is U.S.-centric. It really relies on a Social Security number to work. It also has some mandatory fields for "state," meaning U.S. state, so possessions in other countries could be a problem. Otherwise, it's a solid, affordable solution to a tough problem.

Legacy Locker

The online service Legacy Locker specializes in passing on your digital account information after you die. What sets it apart from other online services is its thorough verification process, which starts with someone reporting your death.

Some online digital afterlife services simply send you an email prompt that you must reply to every so often to say, "Still alive!" If you don't reply to several emails in a row over a period of time, the service assumes you've kicked the bucket. Other services check your Twitter and Facebook accounts for activity. No activity? Well, obviously you're dead! Legacy Locker takes a lot more precautions than some of these competitors.

When you first sign up for Legacy Locker, you have to enter the names of two verifiers who both must confirm that you are incapacitated or deceased, and for the latter, they have to provide a death certificate. Legacy Locker won't hand out any information until the criteria are met.

Legacy Locker also lets you name a beneficiary for different accounts, so you can specify who gets what information. You might pass on the digital keys to your blog, for example, to your blog collaborators while giving your PayPal account info to your significant other. Each beneficiary also has to prove his or her identity to Legacy Locker.

LastPass (Password Manager)

LastPass is another excellent password manager, and you could easily pass on your digital life accounts to a trusted beneficiary by giving him or her your LastPass login.

PasswordBox (Password Manager)

When you first set up PasswordBox, you'll find an option to provide the name and email address of a beneficiary for your passwords. The feature is called Legacy Vault. Upon your death, the beneficiary has to provide the company with a death certificate, which slows down the process of transferring the passwords slightly, but does make it a good, safe, reliable way to pass on those passwords.

V. TAKE-AWAYS

- Don't leave your loved ones in the lurch regarding your digital life after you pass away.
- Choose a method for passing on your online account passwords.
- Assign a beneficiary or multiple beneficiaries who will inherit your online logins.
- Ask your beneficiaries if they are willing to accept the duties of taking over your digital life.
- Explicitly tell your beneficiaries, in an email that you CC to yourself, exactly what you would like them to do with your various accounts, and any special instructions for how they will access them.
- Check the information you have given your beneficiaries annually by revising and resending the email containing the information about what to do with your digital life in the event of an emergency

---

- Additional Content -

My Digital Afterlife Solution

Here's my personal solution for how I intend to pass on my passwords and other important digital life information. I don't necessarily recommend other people take this same approach, but I can at least explain my thinking and why I chose this method over others.

I use the Dashlane password manager, and I intend to give the keys to it to my beneficiary after I die. I've put into my smartphone half the login information needed to get into Dashlane. The other half of the login information I've sent to my beneficiary, who also knows the passcode on my smartphone.

When I set up this strategy, I sent my beneficiary an email with the subject line "emergency info."

The message contains a little bit of preamble, such as a word or two on why he should save this email, and then lists detailed instructions regarding how to find the username and password for Dashlane on my phone. Some of the information on my phone is itself cryptic, so the email contains instructions on how to find and decode it.

The message goes on to say, "Dashlane is a password manager that stores probably 75 percent of my logins. Not everything is in Dashlane, but the email addresses are, so you could conceivably do a password recovery from any site that isn't in Dashlane."

Part of the appeal of this solution is it doesn't involve any other companies or legalities. There's no need to provide a death certificate or sign any paperwork. He gets the passwords, end of story.

I like the treasure hunt aspect, though. My beneficiary has to jump through a couple of hoops—finding that old email, unlocking the phone, decoding the information—to get to my digital life. I don't want it to be too straightforward (I wouldn't want to tempt him to break into my online accounts while I'm still alive and kicking!) but I do want it to be clear for the day when I am eventually not.

And in the event my beneficiary totally forgets I've set up this system for him, well, he'll get an email from Google three months after I've last logged in granting him access to my Gmail account and reminding him that he can find this other email with instructions for how to get all my other account usernames and passwords from the password manager.

Appendix: Checklists

- Run your tune-up utility at least once a month. You can open your tune-up utility to initiate the process yourself, or schedule tune-ups to occur once a month automatically in the software of your choice. (For more, see Chapter 1.)
- Clear your browser's cache and history both on your desktop and laptop computers, and on your smartphone. You can also schedule a clean-up utility to do this for you once a month.
- Flick through your photo albums on your phone and delete images that you know are backed up elsewhere. Put off this task off for too long, and it becomes much harder to complete. (For more, see Chapter 10.)
- Rotate the music you keep on your phone, meaning remove some playlists and albums and replace them with new ones. After a few times of doing it, you might actually start to look forward to the task. It will become a moment when you stop and appreciate your music collection, flip through old albums you haven't played in ages, and make decisions about what you will load onto your phone and delete from it.

Annual Checklist

- Update your most important online passwords, such as for your email accounts, once a year. Some technology experts recommend doing it more often than that, while others don't think change is necessary at all as long as you use strong and unique passwords on all your sites. I personally think that once a year is both doable and helpful. (For more on passwords, see Chapter 5.)
- Archive older files to a more permanent backup device. These files might be roughly older than three years. It's a good project for New Year's Day or the weekend after. (For more, see Chapter 6.)
- Review your LinkedIn profile once a year to make sure it's up to date so that other people can find you. (For more, see Chapter 13.)
- Review your Facebook app permissions and remove anything that you're no longer actively using. Also review and update your privacy settings and contact information.
- If you're aiming for professionalism online, update your photo no more than once a year.
- Review how you are going to pass on your passwords and online accounts to a beneficiary after you die. If you are leaving instructions for someone else, make sure all the details are still accurate and up to date. (For more, see Chapter 15.)

About the Author

Jill Duffy began writing about organization and productivity when she joined PCMag.com in 2011. Her interest in the topic led to a weekly series called simply Get Organized (www.pcmag.com/get-organized). In April 2013, she spoke at TED@250, a small salon-like version of the TED conference, about how to better manage email.

Duffy is also a software analyst, writing product reviews of apps and programs for productivity, social networking, personal finance management, health, fitness, and several other areas.

Across her career, she has written for newspapers, magazines, and websites since 1998, and was the technical editor for two books by McGraw Hill. Before joining PCMag.com, she was senior editor at the Association for Computing Machinery, a non-profit membership organization for computer scientists and students. She also spent five years as managing editor of *Game Developer* magazine, and as a contributing writer to Gamasutra.com. In 2006, she was named one of the 100 most influential women in the video game industry.

Her writing has appeared in *Popular Science, The San Francisco Examiner*, the BBC's *olive* magazine, DigitalTrends.com, and many other publications. She keeps a personal blog on the side at jilleduffy.com. You can follow her on Twitter @jilleduffy.

You can read more 'Get Organized' tips and tricks every Monday at www.pcmag.com/get-organized.

About the Publisher

For more than 30 years, PC Magazine and PCMag.com have been respected as the Independent Guide to Technology, providing in-depth reviews, tech news, buying guides, opinion, downloads, special features, and much more.

PCMag's analysts and editors produce more than 2,200 reviews per year from PC Labs, the largest and oldest technology testing lab in the industry, covering products ranging from laptops and tablets to printers, smartphones, digital cameras, and beyond. For more information, visit PCMag.com.

CPSIA information can be obtained at www.ICGtesting.com
Printed in the USA
LVOW11s0919121014

408392LV00006B/903/P